THREE MEN
IN A ROOM

THREE MEN IN A ROOM

THE INSIDE STORY

OF POWER AND BETRAYAL

IN AN AMERICAN STATEHOUSE

Seymour P. Lachman

with Robert Polner

THE NEW PRESS

NEW YORK
LONDON

Requests for permission to reproduce selections
from this book should be mailed to:
Permissions Department, The New Press, 38 Greene Street, New York, NY 10013.

Published in the United States by The New Press, New York, 2006
Distributed by W. W. Norton & Company, Inc., New York

LIBRARY OF CONGRESS CATALOGING-IN-PUBLICATION DATA

Lachman, Seymour.
    Three men in a room : the inside story of power and betrayal in an American statehouse /
by Seymour P. Lachman, with Robert Polner.
        p.   cm.
    Includes bibliographical references and index.
    ISBN-13: 978-1-59558-032-0
    ISBN-10: 1-59558-032-8
    1. New York (State). Legislature—Ethics.   2. Political corruption—New York (State)
3. Power (Social sciences)—New York (State)   4. New York (State)—Politics and government—1951—   I. Title: 3 men in a room.   II. Polner, Rob.   III. Title.

JK3474.7.L33   2006
328.747—dc22   2006043336

The New Press was established in 1990 as a not-for-profit alternative to the large, commercial
publishing houses currently dominating the book publishing industry. The New Press operates in the public interest rather than for private gain, and is committed to publishing, in in-
novative ways, works of educational, cultural, and community value that are often deemed
insufficiently profitable.

www.thenewpress.com

Composition by dix!
This book was set in Walbaum MT

Printed in the United States of America

1   3   5   7   9   10   8   6   4   2

For Susan

CONTENTS

FOREWORD

Norman Redlich

The "Three Men in a Room" are, of course, the Governor of New York State, the Speaker of the Assembly (usually a Democrat), and the Majority Leader of the State Senate (usually a Republican). On a very rare occasion, when I was the corporation counsel for Mayor John V. Lindsay, I would be the fourth man in the room. Reading former state senator Seymour Lachman's book, I was struck by the similarity with which legislation was handled more than thirty years ago. The governor's representative would have a group of bills in his hands. As the representative went through each bill, he would place them in one of two piles, those that would go to the Legislature and those that would not. Then he would turn to the legislation that affected New York City. There would be agreement among the three officials as to which of these bills would be passed, which would be rejected, and which would not be considered. No one in the room challenged these decisions. I was amazed by the casual manner in which important legislation was treated by the "three men in the room" and, as Senator Lachman skillfully demonstrates in this important book, apparently very little has changed.

This book attempts to describe the way the legislative system actually works, which will undoubtedly surprise most New Yorkers, who have been led to believe that state senators and members of the Assembly actually do legislative work. The real money, and the power, goes to the Senate and Assembly leadership. The legislators share the financial benefits and public esteem, while doing little. Of course, the system operates as it does for two reasons: district lines are drawn through a sophisticated system whereby the Supreme Court's mandate of "one-person, one-vote" is vitiated. Instead, the lines are drawn politically in order to perpetuate the leadership roles of the legislators. Moreover, fund-raising at all levels of state government, by both political parties, is extensive and is the means by which interested parties can secure the results they seek, a result that benefits all members of the Legislature.

One very important section of the book demonstrates how public authorities, created during the Robert Moses era as a method of funding bridges, tunnels, and highways, came to be abused. Public authorities originally were important as a fair method of removing some of the high costs of highways, bridges, and tunnels from the budget calculations of state and local governments. But by removing these expenses and income from budgets, the taxpayers were deceived into thinking that state budgets were balanced. The authorities were happy to cooperate in this public sleight of hand, since these authorities were run by members who held their positions by virtue of state or city appointment—they were part of the patronage process that perpetuates the power of the "three men in a room." The public took little notice until a fiscal crisis arose—and by then, of course, it was too late.

It is surprising that so little has been written about New York's political process. Perhaps New Yorkers have been lulled into a state of mind whereby attention is focused more on national and local government than on state actions. Senator Lachman's book should awaken New Yorkers to the sham of New York's state government. In his concluding pages, he calls for a constitutional convention, which could, if it were ever adopted, alter the budget process and the drawing of legislative lines. The time is right for renewed consideration of a constitutional convention so that New Yorkers can have the government that they believe exists, and which has been sadly lacking. This book is a long-overdue step in the right direction.

ACKNOWLEDGMENTS

The author would like to thank and acknowledge the following interviewees (through conversations or letter) and notes that they do not necessarily agree with the opinions expressed in this book: Patricia Acompora, Warren Anderson, Frank Barbaro, Jerald Benjamin, James Brennan, Richard Brodsky, Hugh Carey, Alan Chertock, Daniel Chill, Jeremy Creelin, Mario Cuomo, Richard Dollinger, Sandy Galef, Emanuel Gold, David Grandeau, James Hagerty, Alan Hevesi, Blair Horner, Jerry Krechmer, Liz Krueger, Eric Lane, Vincent Leibell, Franz Leichter, Rachel Leon, Albert Lewis, Tarky Lombardi, John Marchi, H. Carl McCall, E.J. McMahon, Manfred Ohrenstein, David Sidikman, Eliot Spitzer, Jeffrey M. Stonecash, Robert Stranieri, and Tom Suozzi.

Though much of this book is based on my personal experiences, it does rely as well on the following publications and organizations: the *New York Times*, the *Economist*, the New York *Daily News*, the *Associated Press*, the *New York Observer*, the *New York Post*, *Newsday*, *Newsweek*, the Albany *Times Union*, the *Staten Island Advance*, the *Syracuse Post-Standard*, the *Rochester Democrat and Chronicle*, the *Village Voice*, the

Elmira Star-Gazette, the *Wall Street Journal,* Common Cause New York, the Manhattan Institute, and the New York Public Interest Research Group.

My additional thanks and appreciation go to the following special friends, without whom the publication of this book would not have been possible: Edith Everett, Robert deRothschild, Ira Rennert, Kenneth J. Bialkin, Mitchell Hochberg, Louis Galperin, Bruce Slovin, Sy Steinberg, and Susanne Emmerich. I would also like to thank Kristin McNulty and Andria Dimaggio, my graduate assistants at Adelphi University, for assistance in the preparation of this manuscript.

Last but not least, thanks to Norman Redlich for helping get the project off the ground. I am especially indebted to my longtime friend and former colleague Murray Polner and also to Adam Simms for their writing, editing, and research contributions, and their advice, patience, and continued friendship. Thanks at The New Press to Andy Hsiao and Jeff Z. Klein. Above all, my personal debt to Robert Polner—for his writing, research, and editing—is enormous. Thanks!

CHAPTER 1

A Can of Worms

Democracy requires decades, even centuries, to take root and flourish. It is a fragile plant. My own state, New York, the Empire State, is learning that it takes just three men in a room to cause devastating harm to a democratic system of governance based on the principles of the Founding Fathers.

I spent nearly a decade as an insider of sorts in the New York State capital, never venturing, however, behind the closed doors where the most and least important deals were made. Before running successfully in a special election for a vacant Senate seat in February 1996 and soon after for a full term, I had been a dean at the City University of New York, where I also taught political science and educational administration to graduate students. I lectured at times about the imperfect dynamics and relative merits of the classic liberal arena so well envisioned by English political theorists of the early eighteenth century, such as John Stuart Mill. Within that arena, conflicting interests—those of business, labor, wealthy and influential individuals, and the broader public—grappled toward compromise that one hoped would benefit the greater good and resemble at least a rough fairness.

As my early years as a New York state senator progressed, those lectures seemed hopeful but naive in some ways. Over time I grew surprised, distressed, and finally repelled by the routine subversion of democratic values and processes in a state that was once America's most progressive and activist, a trailblazer in many aspects of economic development, the nurturing of a middle class, worker rights, public education, public health, and poverty relief.

By the end of 2004, after I had spent nearly nine years in the State Senate representing large chunks of Brooklyn and (following a redistricting) Staten Island, I decided I'd had enough of New York State politics. I took an academic position at Adelphi University on Long Island, returning to my roots in educational administration, political science, and the classroom. My decision not to run for reelection, while the result of much soul-searching on my part, gave me months thereafter to explore and reflect on my experiences.

I hadn't been forced by political considerations to say goodbye to my cushioned (and hardly term-limited) perch in the Legislature. There was little chance I would have been defeated for reelection, and my health was still reasonably good.

Nor was I forced by external conditions of any kind to let go of my ample perquisites and possibilities, which go along with any sitting senator's position, such as media attention, phone calls from the likes of Hillary Rodham Clinton or Charles Schumer, deference accorded by community and business leaders, travel reimbursement stipends, staff assistants, and fulsome paychecks for a job I once viewed as full-time but many of my colleagues treated as part-time, especially the approximately two-thirds who had other jobs. (Moonlighting was never terribly difficult for state legislators, considering that the typical lawmaker's workday when the legislature was in session commonly lasted no more than sixty minutes.)

Indeed, I turned my back on the near certainty of another term in Albany, feeling too keenly the toll that my stay there had taken on my sense of my own integrity and on my character. The chasm between the view I held of myself as collaborative and ethically minded, on one hand, and the expectations of a lockstep political subservience set by arrogant superiors on the other was widening, it seemed, by the minute. I didn't like what was happening to the state government; I didn't like being a veritable puppet, either. I reluctantly came to the conclusion that I couldn't possibly make an important difference—despite occasional successes—by working from within the system.

What was more, I determined that it didn't really matter whether Democrats or Republicans controlled Albany now or in the future, because the place was too rotten at its core. Absent fierce pressure for reform over months and years, neither the members of my party—the Democrats—nor the Republicans were going to bring an open, transparent, contentious, and vital democracy to New York State. Ever.

So I left Albany and turned my attention to researching and assembling this account in hopes of contributing to the groundswell of recent years aimed at bringing change to one of the country's most secretive and misruled statehouses—and to contribute as well to the call for more democratic governance in state capitols around the country.

The time is now.

The United States is a country where the idea of an activist national government has come under unrelenting attack from many well-endowed and conservative quarters. Sometimes for better and sometimes for worse, the United States Congress has increasingly delegated decisions about the use of federal funds to the states to grapple with, as when Bill Clinton ended the New Deal requirement of aiding the needy with welfare; now the states decide who among the needy is worthy of assistance, and what they need to prove about themselves to receive temporary cash benefits.

The motivation for writing this book, the first of its kind by a former New York state senator and academic, is also grounded in my conviction that Americans are entitled to a full-throated voice in politics and an unobstructed window on its dealings, particularly in a world in which quickly transmitted information is power, and undue secrecy—which is antithetical to well-informed choices since it prevents ideas and policies from being debated or debunked—runs rampant in municipal, state, and federal governments. Churchill called democracy the worst form of government except for all the other alternatives. Democracy, however, can always be improved, even if it can't be perfected. The people are entitled to real democracy, rather than merely window dressing or photo ops and public relations, all part of the charade that calls itself democracy. Real democracy is what our soldiers have been asked to fight and perhaps die for in countless wars. For public participation to be short-circuited anywhere within the United States, as I believe is exemplified every day in the Empire State, should be galling and unacceptable—especially while the nation engages, at the cost of terrible loss of life and many billions of dollars, in a grim war sold to the American public as a method of exporting those values to post–Saddam Hussein Iraq.

New Yorkers are not blind to the corruption of their state government. Indeed, a survey of 620 registered voters in 2006 sponsored by the Empire Center for New York State Policy and conducted by the Siena College Research Institute found that 75 percent believe that the ethics of state officials had worsened in the previous five years, while 83 percent said that their elected representatives in Albany fail to represent their interests. The poll also found 68 percent support for substantial checks on their powers, such as term limits, and 74 percent in favor of the creation of a nonpartisan, independent board to determine the number and size of legislative districts every ten years based on the federal population census.

Allow me, then, to put forth in these pages the comparatively modest but extremely important recommendation that we, as citizens, look to our state governments here at home for a restoration and revival of both the idea and the practice of American concepts of good government.

Since early 2002, and to some extent even before, several newspapers across New York State have played a strong and important role in the push for reform, editorializing powerfully about the need for systemic changes of many aspects of New York State's government. Most editorial writers have taken aim at the processes and practices designed to perpetuate the iron grip on decision making held by three largely unaccountable public servants—the Governor, the Assembly Speaker, and the Senate Majority Leader in Albany.

The *New York Times*, for example, began a lengthy string of editorials in February 2002 decrying what the editorial writers correctly termed a usually deadlocked and demoralizing state of affairs in Albany. The paper even assumed an incumbent-wary stance in its candidate endorsements, determined to see the entrenched status quo shaken up or at least sent a message: make dramatic changes or get out of the way.

By the eve of the legislative primaries of September 2004,

many other editorial boards around the state also were exhorting readers to vote against the incumbent, whatever his or her history of bringing home the bacon to the district or degree of influence in the Albany hierarchy, and regardless of the caliber of his or her opponent.

The mounting frustration expressed by editorial boards both conservative and liberal is understandable. Office holders in Albany face no term limits and are rarely voted out of office because of extraordinary powers of incumbency accorded to them in a self-serving system of rules and practices geared to the cultivation of funds and "safe" districts.

The *Staten Island Advance* ran an op-ed piece of mine as part of a full-page editorial. My essay had originally appeared in *Newsday*, another newspaper that has used its editorial voice to denounce the Legislature's close-to-the-vest mode of operating. My essay amounted to a summary of one Democrat's call for radical surgery in how Albany was permitted to operate. That it was soon reprinted as an editorial in as independent a newspaper as the *Advance* illuminated, to me, just how disenchanted with state government many people of all political allegiances had become.

Then came another important development. In July 2004, New York University's Brennan Center for Justice released a report (more about it later; to many it was a turning point) concluding that New York's Legislature was the most dysfunctional in the nation—the country's "worst," as the accompanying press release put it. In the accurate words of the extremely detailed, state-by-state comparative analysis: "New York State's legislative process is broken."

New York's probably isn't the worst legislature in the United States; arguably one might look to the historically corrupt and colorful one in Louisiana in the wake of Hurricane Katrina in

August 2005 for indications of an even less effective legislature (albeit one all but abandoned in its darkest hours by the federal officials and agencies responsible for domestic defenses). But New York, with its twenty-year losing streak of late budgets from 1984 to 2004, has fallen a long way from its twentieth-century heyday—the eras of the Depression and the New Deal, when Alfred Smith, Franklin D. Roosevelt, and Herbert Lehman were governors—to the bottom percentile of state legislatures, right down there with Louisiana's.

Nassau County executive Thomas Suozzi, a Democrat, launched in 2004 a "Fix Albany" campaign. Under this banner, he successfully targeted for defeat a Long Island incumbent who he said was too close to the Democratic Assembly Speaker and would never buck the Speaker's apparent complacency about ballooning Medicaid expenses and inefficiencies, which create pressure on suburban counties to raise their property taxes. Suozzi argued that constituents on Long Island and around the state deserved a greater voice in Albany through their elected state representatives. The challenger Suozzi backed in the primary was someone he said would seek to confront the problems in Albany with more vigor and independence than the longtime incumbent. Although incumbents, scandalously, almost never lose in New York State, this time one actually did. Suozzi's reform-oriented candidate removed a well-liked and competent assemblyman from the Legislature as a means of sending a message to the Democratic Assembly Speaker that the time for reforms, and not cosmetic ones, was growing near.

In 2005, some reforms were actually adopted in response to the public mood, editorials, political activities, and the defeat of the Suozzi-targeted candidate. Additionally, longtime Republican state senator Nancy Lorraine Hoffman of Syracuse fell to an insurgent campaign that was aimed at sending a similar reform message to the powerful Senate Majority Leader, Joseph Bruno, a Republican who represents Rensselaer County and Saratoga Springs. Meanwhile, State Senator Nick Spano of Westchester County, the Deputy Majority Leader under Bruno, survived the challenge, but by a mere eighteen votes. There was no question that reforming Albany was a political issue to be reckoned with.

Still another sign revealed that its time had come: both Republican and Democratic incumbents who had never dared to broach the issue now gave it at least lip service. Reformers are "morning glories," as George Washington Plunkett, the quotable Tammany Hall politician of a different era, once put it. They "looked lovely in the mornin' and withered up in a short time—while the regular machines went on flourishin' forever, like fine old oaks."

What resulted, in 2005, was a much-publicized series of ethics and rules reforms, but these were modest in scope and some were even regressive, though the minor attempts to democratize the two houses of the Legislature were at least notable by Albany standards.

It nonetheless became ever clearer to me and other observers that the dysfunction and undemocratic governance in many American states demanded continuing attention. Americans should never accept the gross abrogation of their democratic ideals, either in their state capitals or in Washington, where cabals, corporations, an army of lobbyists, and an array of special interests have turned Congress and the executive branch into a feeding trough for the richest and most influential interests. New York's Legislature and many other state legislatures, which should be a bulwark against harmful federal actions or federal indifference, languish, too, from the effects of brazen patronage, corruption, boondoggles, inefficiency, insularity, knee-jerk aversion to innovation, and carefully rigged procedures to protect the decision makers and those who endear themselves to them.

Greater attention to the problem can at the very least become an important reminder of the great power and potential of state legislatures over the lives of the citizens.

I am seventy-one years old—and perpetually surprised to remember I am not, say, thirty-five anymore. I like to tell younger men and women to seize the day. Of all the things that fly, life goes fastest.

My family's first apartment was in the South Bronx, and when I was one year old, my parents changed boroughs. I grew up in Brooklyn. My father, Louis, had been a seminary student in his native Poland. My mother was Sarah, and also from Poland. The two arrived together by ship and passed through New York's legendary Ellis Island between the world wars.

My father, a thoughtful man, briefly owned a candy store that closed during the Depression. My mother, a homemaker, and my father dedicated their lives to their children's well-being. Education was an important part of this objective.

Most immigrant families have a story of hardship from which later generations can draw lessons and inspiration. Mine did, too. My parents lost siblings and relatives in the Holocaust and dreamed, like many American Jews, of moving to Israel. At one point, my father bought an orange grove in what is now the center of Tel Aviv with what little savings he had, only to sell it off prior to World War II to help bring a brother and the brother's family from Poland.

My parents were in their mid-forties when my mother became pregnant with me. Their firstborn son had died when he was five from a burst appendix; a doctor misdiagnosed the dis-order and told them to take the ailing boy home and give him an enema. Then as now, a fresh-off-the-boat immigrant couple didn't usually question the wisdom of a physician, and in their case tragedy resulted.

After the horrible loss of their first child, a second, my brother, was born a year later. It took another five years before I showed up, giving them two boys to raise.

But the death of my brother challenged my parents' spirit for the rest of their days. My father died when I was just twenty-two years old, and my mother died not long thereafter, living just long enough to meet the woman who would become my beloved wife, Susan. For any young person starting out in life, it's terrible to lose both parents. It is surely more difficult for a son to handle in his twenties than when he is older and more established, and with a family of his own.

The early loss of my parents will always remain with me, as well as a deep, hard-to-describe feeling of obligation to the older brother I knew only from framed black-and-white pho-tographs and family remembrances. I felt an obligation to be, in how I conduct my personal and public duties, the type of person he might have been if he had lived. At the heart of that feeling is a desire to be a reliable breadwinner for my wife and children, religiously faithful, public-spirited, mindful of and helpful to those in need, and, yes, as ethical a person as hu-manly possible.

As a young man I taught social studies at Thomas Jefferson and Lafayette High Schools in Brooklyn to the children of im-migrant and working-class families. Years later I earned a doc-torate from New York University, was appointed to the New York City Board of Education at age thirty-five, and eventually was elected by my peers to serve as its president.

I was drawn into the community battles over the direction of New York City's public school system, the nation's largest. I helped guide the board through one of the school system's most volatile periods, the early and mid-1970s. The period came shortly after poor, minority parents in neighborhoods such as Ocean Hill–Brownsville had demanded and obtained a stronger voice in the operation of their children's troubled and segregated schools.

The 1954 Supreme Court decision in *Brown v. Board of Education of Topeka* had outlawed "separate but equal" schools, stirring African American protests around the country, including in Brooklyn and Harlem, and demands for improved educational opportunities for their children. By the 1960s, black-white politics had taken America by storm. Sit-ins in the South to end segregation gave way to protests to integrate and make more equitable New York City's public schools, which were also segregated, not by legislative law but rather by residential patterns and practices, including redlining, blockbusting, and school district gerrymandering. Middle-class New Yorkers, mainly whites of European ancestry, were leaving the city in droves for the booming suburbs—one million people between 1955 and 1965 alone; zoning and racial steering were used to try to keep blacks and Hispanics out of suburbia. If anyone still doubted that a national movement toward equality was under way, Congress passed a drumbeat of civil rights legislation between 1964 and 1968, including fair housing laws.

In New York, minority parents' demands for a voice in their children's education was galvanized in Albany when a hurried and historic law decentralized the New York City school system into what became thirty-two semi-autonomous community school districts, each with its own elected school board. The voting process for school board elections under the legislation was badly flawed; the complex, difficult-to-comprehend "weighted" system for determining elections of community school board candidates allowed organized interests, such as the teachers union and religious groups, to gain control of many local boards. The New York City Board of Education retained, under the legislation, great powers over policies, purchasing, security, and school performance largely through its appointment of a schools chancellor. The chancellor, however, became a convenient political target of whoever happened to be mayor, and sometimes of the formidable education unions as well.

During the rocky transition from a single central board to a constellation of community school district boards, I sought with some success to integrate the ranks of the central schools administration, something that had never been done. At the same time, the board accorded civil rights for the first time to students—the right, for one, to appeal a suspension by the principal. That was among the most memorable achievements I helped bring about.

The results of this period of massive change were imperfect, but the inauguration of a democratically driven system cooled emotions and blunted the potential for violent disruption and further deterioration across a system of about one million mostly poor students. Because the structural changes had stemmed in large measure from grassroots protests, the school system was given by all parties a chance to prove itself.

Throughout my tenure at the Board of Education, I learned (sometimes the hard way) that the voices of the public must be listened to and that our decisions, sometimes mistaken, sometimes wise, were reached not by consensus or by mandate from a select few, but rather by public argument, intense discussions, open and public hearings—indeed, all the trappings of a democratic society struggling to do the right thing. In much the same spirit, community planning boards were introduced across New York City during the mayoralty of John Lindsay, and beginning in the 1960s they too became an essential avenue of public involvement—a source of information and advice about community needs that had been overlooked; the boards exist to this day.

In 1989 the U.S. Supreme Court ruled that the existence and operations of another major city panel—the Board of Estimate, a smoke-filled back room at City Hall where huge land-use decisions were bartered and brokered—violated the constitutional principle of one person, one vote. It was scrapped in favor of a much larger and more representative City Council, with fifty-one members. Adding to the democratization of city government, the voters have stepped up in subsequent years to create such things as the New York City Independent Budget Office, a key oversight board independent of the mayor and the council, and two-term limits for the mayor, the two other citywide officials (public advocate and city comptroller), the borough presidents, and all fifty-one council members. I should note that when each of these changes was coming down the pike, incumbents and other critics often said that the reforms would lead to paralysis and chaos in city government. But we live in a democratic society and, lo and behold, democracy, while never neat and trim, brought in fresh ideas, new leadership, and benefits, where before there had been a hidebound system stuck in some self-serving habits and, often enough, corruption.

Years after I left the Board of Education, I taught political science and education law. Still, my knowledge of Albany's arcane workings was theoretical. Looking back at my career as a state senator, I realized that I had been naive. I had believed in the separation of powers, the implicit if not explicit authority of the voters, and the classical theory of the democratic arena, in which competing interests offset and blunted one another's reach, creating a rough equilibrium and quality of fairness. How wrong I was. I discovered firsthand that the reality in Albany was quite different from the theory I had taught in the classroom.

I first chose to run for the New York State Legislature in February 1996 in a legislative district initially covering parts of Brooklyn (and later parts of Staten Island as well). After first winning the backing of reformist Democratic assemblyman Frank Barbaro, borough president Howard Golden, and the powerful Democratic organization in Kings County (Brooklyn), I ran for and won a special midterm election. That November, I ran successfully for the first of four full two-year terms.

It took me about a year to begin to see the New York State Legislature for what it was and still is—a Potemkin village whose elaborate and impressive housing and rhetorical high dudgeon hid its lack of integrity, democracy, and, too often, substance.

As I was slowly learning how things worked, I traveled more than three hours from my home in Brooklyn to spend many a day and night in Albany. The more I grew to know about the inscrutable operations carried on there—unknown to most outsiders—the more I grew determined to keep from becoming too compromised. I tried to protect my independence, sometimes at the price of giving up a chance to rise quickly in the ranks. Still, at other times, admittedly, I participated in voting for things I did not in my heart or head support.

Like anyone in the Legislature, initially I didn't want to do anything that could cause difficulty every two years when I came up for reelection. I wanted to be accepted by my colleagues and amass some influence that might benefit my district and political aspirations. I was ambitious enough to dream of one day serving in Congress.

Within a short time of my arrival in the State Senate, I was appointed to the Senate's Finance Committee. Soon I began to vote my own way on important issues of concern to me and to my constituents. Very shortly thereafter, I was approached by a senior member of the Democratic Party who said, "Listen, you can either support the Democratic leadership and rise to the very top, or be an independent who votes on principle, and sink to the bottom."

I felt somewhat like the way Tom Suozzi's handpicked reform candidate, Charles Lavine, must have felt in 2004 when he was asked to cast an immediate vote for the reappointment of Sheldon Silver, the Democrat who was the longtime Speaker of the Assembly. He did as requested, explaining later to a reporter that even though he had run on a platform of independence from the certain-to-win Speaker, he determined that he would have no effectiveness from the very start of his tenure if he stood on principle and voted against the man at the pinnacle of a top-down organization.

In 1999, something happened that solidified my growing unease with the way the State Legislature worked. Assembly Speaker Sheldon Silver, along with Senator Martin Connor, the Democratic Minority Leader in the Republican-led Senate chamber, joined with Republican Senate Majority Leader Joseph Bruno to do away with the so-called commuter tax—the tiny, fractional income tax on suburban commuters to New York City. The cost to individual taxpayers of this levy was minute, but collectively the tax produced between $350 million and $500 million a year for perennially cash-strapped New

York City. And as was well known, the commuter tax helped pay for so many of the city-subsidized services and amenities that commuters depended on, benefited from, and enjoyed, from policing and firefighting to world-renowned museums, legendary parks, and nonprofit research hospitals of the highest quality.

The rationale of Silver and Connor in seeking to eliminate the commuter tax was to help a Democratic Senate candidate with his uphill attempt to gain a seat representing a suburban district in Rockland County. So it was merely a political maneuver on their part, though diametrically opposed to the interests of their own New York City constituents. I refused to back the bill; I confess it was a political no-brainer for me, since virtually no constituent in my district was bound to disagree with my urban-protective stance.

Even so, many of my Democratic colleagues later told me I had been mistaken to resist the political might and will of the Democratic leadership; there had been no way to stop that particular juggernaut, so my vote was only symbolic, they told me, and would only boomerang to my political and personal detriment. While I lobbied my Democratic colleagues in the Assembly to save the commuter tax, most Democrats in that Democratic-led chamber predictably followed Assembly Speaker Silver's lead and voted to kill the important levy. Some who didn't get on the bandwagon were given special dispensation. Others, like myself, went off the reservation without a pass—hardly a brave feat, but unusual all the same in Albany.

It's also a fact, to my lasting dismay, that the Democratic Minority Leader of the Senate himself, Martin Connor of Brooklyn, had pushed to eliminate the commuter tax, too, as did his reform-minded future successor, David Paterson of Harlem. At the time, I asked Senator Paterson why. After all, New York

City had depended on a commuter tax at least since the infamous fiscal crisis of the 1970s, and the tax was much smaller than many believed was needed to offset the mass exodus from the city to the suburbs in those years. (Suburban legislators had made sure it remained tiny in 1971, catering to an ever-growing suburban voting population at the expense of a troubled city that had traditionally been the fiscal engine for the state.) Paterson smiled at me. He leaned toward Connor and implied that he had to go along with the vote because of the Democratic leadership of both houses.

Ironically, despite the killing of the commuter tax by decisive margins in both houses, the Republican candidate in Rockland County won anyway, with the support of Republicans Joseph Bruno and Governor George Pataki.

The commuter tax fiasco, typical of Albany's ways, crystallized for me the reality that the Legislature's leadership ran the government much like the stacked Presidium of the Soviet regime. From early on in my tenure, I witnessed legislative leaders changing the votes of an elected official right out in the open when they didn't agree with his or her opinion; that was, they felt, their prerogative. I came to see that such a thing was not uncommon. Also widespread: "proxy" voting, which allowed legislators' committee votes to be registered in their absence by their party leaders.

As a result of my vote against killing the commuter tax, I was seen as too autonomous of the Senate Democratic leadership, and even idiosyncratic.

Look, I am no saint, no martyr, and never looked at myself that way. I, too, compromised some of my personal standards simply to be able to function with a reasonable degree of effectiveness for my district in the tightly controlled halls of power. I also realize now that many legislators felt as I do, but believed there was nothing they could do, given the rigid Albany hierarchy. Yet Albany remains a cosmic black hole, a place where most politicians, Republicans and Democrats alike, soon find they cannot be influential or even hold a bit part when it comes to important decisions.

"If people understand what is going on in Albany today," said former Governor Mario Cuomo in a 2005 interview with me, "they would say it is a can of worms."

Consider these recent falls from grace:

• Guy Velella, longtime Bronx/Westchester state senator and leader in the Republican Party, pleaded guilty in 2004 to one count of bribery and agreed to serve up to a year in jail (in the end he served six months). Despite the seriousness of the charges—Velella was alleged to have pocketed $137,000 in bribes to help steer public works contracts through state agencies—Joseph Bruno raised about $150,000 from the GOP legislators' campaign funds to pay the legal bills of a besieged political insider.

• In 2003, an assemblywoman, Gloria Davis, resigned and served a brief jail sentence after being caught accepting cash bribes. The Bronx Democrat also accepted free rides between Albany and the Bronx in vans owned by the Correctional Services Corporation, a business that received an extension of its state contract with her assistance.

• Another assemblyman resigned after a legislative ethics commission issued a report—never subsequently released—assailing his alleged use of public travel stipends for personal errands. The secrecy surrounding the potentially embarrassing ethics report and the fact that no felony charges were ever brought may have helped the assemblyman recover from his predicament. He ran for his seat again three months later and easily won. He was also given an assist, no doubt, by legislative redistricting, as it resulted in the exclusion from the district of the home of his most serious challenger, so the challenger couldn't run against him.

The leader of the Kings County Democratic Party organization, and deputy Speaker of the Assembly, Clarence Norman Jr., was found guilty in the fall of 2005 as a result of an investigation by the Brooklyn district attorney, Charles Hynes. Norman was convicted of soliciting illegal campaign contributions and covering up his actions. He had been tried, as the *New York Times* reported on September 28, 2005, for allegedly soliciting from a lobbyist contributions of $7,423.30 in 2000 and $5,400 in 2002—well above the state's $3,100 contribution limit—and then trying to hide the contributions. At the beginning of 2006, Norman was ordered to spend the next two to six years in prison, though he has been free pending appeal, and he won a round in one of his legal battles when, in March, a state Supreme Court jury cleared him of charges that he had double-billed for travel expenses. Brooklyn state Supreme Court justice Martin Marcus rejected his plea to be forgiven, calling him "devious and manipulative."

The gross misapplication of power by Democrats as well as by Republicans in positions of authority is hardly limited to Clarence Norman's activities. After a Brooklyn Surrogate Court judge was removed for awarding to a friend a total of $8.6 million in legal fees for handling the affairs of people who died without wills, the State Legislature stepped in with a curious "reform." It approved a bill that added a second, and unnecessary, judge's seat to the Surrogate Court for Brooklyn, and ensured the position would not be filled by voters electing judges in the primary and general election; rather, the judge would be appointed by the Brooklyn Democratic Party organization. As columnist Joyce Purnick reported in the *Times* in September 2005, the bill was approved on June 23, 2005. It set the effective date for the creation of the additional judgeship as August 1, 2005—eighteen days after the New York State Board of Elections permits sending in petitions for the Democratic primary ballot.

The additional judgeship was clearly a function of the usual patronage deals on the courts statewide, with the same bill also creating extra judgeships in courts in New York City and northern New York counties. Governor Pataki received the power to appoint fourteen new judges on the Court of Claims. More Supreme Court judges were also created. Republican and Democratic leaders in Albany—Pataki among them—were up to their old power-rationing tricks. Thus did one major scandal beget another in classic Albany fashion, all in the name of reform.

It would be unfair to single out some of Albany's politicians. But they should set a higher standard. Pataki, for example, has taken full and continuing advantage of Virginia's campaign finance laws, liberal even in comparison to New York's notoriously lax restrictions on raising and spending campaign funds, to ramp up for a possible (though unlikely) run for president.

In addition, the Senate Majority Leader, Bruno, may or may not have been happy to give his son, at one time an Albany lobbyist, his ear on important matters facing the Legislature despite the complexities and questions that this personal-professional relationship could possibly raise. Some background: in 1995, there was a push to clear the way for Las Vegas–style casinos in the Catskills. Pataki introduced a bill authorizing five casinos there, which would be given to Indian tribes to settle their land claims against the state. But the Governor yanked the bill after it encountered opposition in the Legislature and complicating court decisions. Pataki then offered a bill that would have allowed one casino only, to settle a claim by the Akwesasne Mohawks. The Assembly passed it, but the Senate held back, saying it wanted to green-light three casinos to generate more revenue and satisfy more tribes—including one represented by the son of Bruno. What is the average person to think about motivations for that decision? Could it be another case of favoritism, or mere coincidence? Whatever the truth, the results were of a type familiar to observers of the Legislature: inaction, since the Legislature did nothing. In 2006, Bruno's son Kenneth gave up his lobbying job and started to work as an independent attorney.

Inaction, deliberate paralysis, doesn't come out of thin air. It is a choice that arises, at least in part, from the fact that most legislators can't or won't rock the boat stewarded by the Governor, Assembly Speaker, and Senate Majority Leader, and the private interests that successfully play up to them. The unconnected, unrelated, average citizen or civic-minded entity, voluntary or private, doesn't really stand a chance of influencing the state's course. They certainly can't depend on their Assembly members or senators to have the audacity to go up against the leadership, or even the authority to make a difference. Unless, that is, their elected representative wants to endanger his or her chances for reelection to their currently $79,500-a-year jobs and annual stipends of $9,000 to $40,000. (Some are seeking a raise to push their legislative salary past $100,000 a year as soon as possible.)

In 2004, my last year in Albany, the legislature failed to pass its budget on time for the twentieth year in a row. Here again was stagnation. As a result, low-income teenagers did not immediately have the summer jobs they or their parents had counted on. Poor people did not get the tax rebates they were promised. Thousands of college students from struggling working-class families could not know how much tuition aid they might get come the fall semester.

Nor would there be a plan that year, despite a federal mandate and warnings of a loss of $150 million in reimbursement, for upgrading the state's century-old voting machines—that, too, would have to wait. By January 2006, the State Legislature faced a Justice Department threat of a lawsuit over delays, more than five years after the 2000 presidential election debacle in Florida had prompted a congressional act requiring every state to upgrade voting machines and systems. New York's modernization plan arrived too late for new equipment to be put in place for the November 2006 elections, including the gubernatorial contest. The Justice Department said that New York State, which critics contended was too swayed by voting-technology vendors and especially their lobbyists, had the worst record in the country when it came to complying with the mandate. Finally, in March 2006, the Justice Department sued, making an example of New York.

New York State also received scathing criticism in early 2006 from a State Supreme Court judge over its clubhouse-controlled system for selecting jurists to run, usually uncontested, for their seats on the bench. The judge called the state's selection system one of the least fair in the country, ruling that a party's judicial candidates must be chosen instead by a nonpartisan blue-ribbon panel before being placed on the ballot. And he said that until the Legislature saw fit to come up with such a merit-based selection process, he himself would screen the qualifications of those in the legal profession seeking to run in the primaries, irrespective of their record of campaign contributions to the political party organizations.

Stalling is a time-honored tactic, but in New York State it has had the effect of undermining public confidence in the process. For five years in a row there had been no change in the state's persistently low minimum wage of $5.15 an hour, and in 2004 it appeared that things would be no different, thanks to a divided Legislature and a politically timed gubernatorial veto of a bill to raise it. The Assembly could not and the Senate would not vote to override Pataki's veto, with the Republican presidential convention coming to New York State that summer and the three-term Republican Governor hinting at presidential ambitions. The minimum wage was finally raised in a special session after the reelection of President George W. Bush, though incrementally and without regard to issues of enforcement.

Badly needed reform of the campaign finance system and lobbying rules, which stand up poorly to many other states' processes, went unconsidered, too, in this late-budget anniversary year of 2004. While most legislators in Albany now agreed that the three-decade-old Rockefeller drug laws, among the harshest in the nation, needed to be watered down or thrown out, the New York State Legislature again put off amending the draconian laws, finally enacting only minor modifications after the 2004 election (potentially affecting a maximum of a thousand prisoners out of sixteen thousand predominantly black and Latino people locked up under the laws, often for first-time, nonviolent offenses). "When the pressure mounted to the point of affecting their political careers, politicians reacted," Anthony Papa, a former Rockefeller law prison inmate, activist, and author (*15 to Life: How I Painted My Way to Freedom*), wrote later on the *Gotham Gazette* Web site, "a huge applause was heard. Politicians felt the pressure easing. Individuals who had called for reform began backing off. After all those years of fighting, a change had occurred." Six months after the changes, Papa wrote, only eighty-six inmates had been set free, with prosecutors determined only to reduce sentences, at best. So Albany's drug-law reforms were largely symbolic, since they were rarely applied. The vast bulk of people eligible to petition for early release remain behind bars. The Governor and the Legislature applauded themselves just the same.

The core of dysfunction, the sense of a body handcuffed to immediate election calculations and other expediencies, resides in the fact that although there are 212 legislators in Albany, just three men hold virtually all the cards; the Governor, the Speaker, and the Majority Leader, known as the Big Three. They determine the details of the budget, which happens to be the fourth largest in the nation, behind the federal government's and that of the states of California and Texas. They hire most of the staff, including those who draft most bills. The leaders also dispense committee chairs and membership assignments, assign office and office furniture, and run all the services that legislators rely on, from publications to payroll. Should a member of one of the two houses author a piece of legislation, the leader decides which committee it goes to, whether it is passed in the committee, and when or even if it gets passed out for a (predetermined) vote on the floor.

The leader of each house can stop a bill from advancing at virtually any point in its journey toward becoming law. This power is accepted and acceded to by most legislators, who realize they can probably remain in office comfortably as long as they don't challenge the system. As noted, legislators don't even have to stick around for legislative sessions, as Senate committee votes can be made for them under a legally questionable proxy-voting system.

Much to my chagrin and that of many others, dozens of bills are typically put in front of members' faces with only hours or even minutes left to go before the floor vote, and with no time to consider them. Would it cause "chaos," as some contend, if Assembly members and senators were given a reliable voice within the leadership-and-legislative-whip system in the process of debating and passing bills and budgets on behalf of their state and constituents? It would not. But it is not allowed.

This Presidium-like scenario periodically brings on revolts. Michael Bragman, an assemblyman from Onondaga County, tried in 2000 to oust Silver from his leadership perch, arguing that drastic changes in the operation of the Assembly were urgently needed. It was what some newspapers called a "coup attempt"; perhaps he was motivated and inspired by Bruno's ascension during a similar battle royal in 1994, when Bruno defeated then–Majority Leader Ralph Marino. Silver pounced, stripping Bragman of his high-level position as Majority Leader in the Assembly and demoting several of his co-conspirators. Other members were threatened with challengers in their next election if they did not support Silver's reappointment. However, Silver did make some minor changes after Bragman's failure to oust him.

So Silver was restored to the powerful post of Speaker, with the vast majority of Democrats voting for him so as to avoid being ostracized and punished themselves.

Bragman went from being one of the most senior people in Albany's hierarchy to becoming a pariah there. He resigned from the Assembly in December 2001. He had stuck out his neck in a Legislature in which the leaders have no one within their houses to check or countervail their powers, and his head was chopped off.

There have been less dramatic but serious efforts to restore democracy to Albany since I left office, such as a lawsuit brought by a Republican assemblyman from Newburgh, Tom Kirwan, and a Democratic senator from Manhattan, Liz Krueger. That lawsuit challenged the ingenious ways that the leadership in Albany has cut the legs out from under the minority parties in both houses (Democrats in the Senate, Republicans in the Assembly) and thus unfairly and unconstitutionally abrogated the right of one person, one vote as it applies to the minority legislators' constituents (some 14.5 million voters in all). In late 2005, a state Supreme Court judge ruled that the lawsuit, a push for a more open and fairly run Legislature, could proceed on some of its main arguments. It is no coincidence, however, that one of the sponsors of the suit, Krueger, had her newsletter censored, as some of my Democratic colleagues and I had at other times.

There are, too, ongoing attempts to make a difference through the polls—which for the Democrats in the Senate means trying to win enough seats to take away the majority rule of the Republicans in that body. So far, these electoral efforts by Democrats to win back the Senate one seat at a time have been modestly successful in some instances and faltering in others. Even if they are successful, it is doubtful that Democrats in the leadership positions of both chambers would seek to dilute and disperse their own power—a necessary prerequisite on the road to restoring democracy.

Therefore, only a historic constitutional convention, which would throw open the state's charter, can change the governing structure to make it more accountable, transparent, and representative, and can have the desired result. (Much more about this later.) Change cannot be brought about from within the Legislature.

This is a state capital that has even seen fit to turn a deaf ear and blind eye to the ruling of its highest court, the Court of Appeals, to overhaul and make fairer its process for doling out billions of dollars in school aid (based on the grassroots Campaign for Fiscal Equity's ten-year court case that current state aid processes deny students' right, under the state constitution, to a "sound, basic education").

During my time in Albany, I had a front-row seat for this sad spectacle. I observed an American statehouse's chronic dysfunction up close, in the venue where preordained decisions were played out. The following chapters combine the intimate knowledge of someone who worked in the clubby ranks of state politics with the analysis and, I hope, insights of a longtime academic and educational administrator. I feel an urgent necessity, and even a sense of mission, to return democracy to the Empire State.

CHAPTER 2

Like a Meeting of the Supreme Soviet

State Senator Liz Krueger, one of my former legislative colleagues, says she may never forget her first committee meeting after she was elected in a special election in February 2002. It served as a kind of introduction to the peculiar habits of Albany. No one other than she and the panel's chair was present, she recalled. Most of the seats were still empty at future meetings that she, like her colleagues, had been elected to attend faithfully. She remembered wondering, "Where the heck was everyone else?"

It was no different for me or for any of the other minority party members of New York's lower and upper houses of the Legislature—the Democrats in the Republican-controlled Senate like me, or the Republicans in the Democratic-controlled Assembly.

And the odd thing about it was, this relatively powerless condition was much the same for majority members of both of Albany's houses as well. They were equally subservient to the leaders of their legislative branches.

Outside the irregular lines of the New York state legislator's election district, beyond the trappings of his or her elected office, the Albany legislator quickly learned his or her place in the rigid hierarchy that passes for democracy.

To be sure, we could, as legislators, attend as many committee meetings as our hearts desired. But for many of us, there was really no point. We were expected simply to give our party's ranking committee member our proxy to vote any way that the house leader advised him or her. At the same time, the proxy ensured that the committee meetings had on paper enough attendance, or a legal quorum, for the committee's decisions about bills to count. As individuals, we knew we could not influence legislation or force our own bills to a vote.

Citizens weren't likely to know of their representatives' velvet-handcuffed condition nor many lawmakers' frequent absence from legislative committee meetings, because, unlike the Brooklyn elementary school of my youth, our attendance wasn't recorded, and our proxies—which Bob Freedman of the New York State Committee on Open Government, an oversight office, has publicly described as constitutionally dubious at best—misleadingly indicated our presence to anyone who bothered to check our voting records.

We could show up for the sessions of the full house if we chose to but, amazingly, that wasn't required, either, due to a separate and equally objectionable procedure known as empty-seat voting, in which a senator's absence basically indicated an affirmative vote on whichever bill the leader favored as long as he or she briefly signed in before or during the day with the Senate clerk. At the state level, just five other legislative chambers in the country used a system of absentee voting, and only one of them was comparable to New York's. Public outrage and minor rule changes in 2005 limited (but did not end) absentee voting, much to the distress of those legislators who unabashedly felt that they should not be required to attend debates in which their votes might be required.

Another charade that many legislators excelled at was attaching their names to as many unobjectionable, apple-pie bills as possible—those that merely renamed a street in their legislative district, say, or honored a recently deceased constituent. And they regularly got their names appended to potentially popular bills they knew would never pass the other house.

When elections rolled around, otherwise impotent legislators pointed to the many bills they had thus sponsored. But these "one-house" bills were crafted not to pass the other house and become law but simply to impress voters or wealthy individuals and interest groups that could be counted on to contribute big money to their campaigns. "Sorry, voters," was the basic message; "though we tried to cut your income taxes, increase school aid, punish criminals, assist small businesses, or increase the pensions of union members, our vile opponents in the other party just wouldn't go for it." In 2002, of 16,892 bills introduced, 4.4 percent were passed—the lowest proportion in any statehouse in the land.

Still, the legislators who played along with this transparent game—on some level it was impossible not to—could hope to garner prestige and lifetime job security in the marble corridors of the State Capitol. As a reward, they were apt to receive a prestigious committee assignment or see their names appended to leadership bills destined to become actual law through negotiations among the Senate Majority Leader, the Assembly Speaker, and the Governor and their senior staffs.

Rarely did any of the committees on which I served at different times—including transportation; aging; consumer protection; corporations, authorities, and commissions; crime victims, crimes, and corrections; education; finance; and higher education—hold public hearings on proposed legislation. What would be the point of hearing from constituents and experts on any given issue, one might reasonably ask, if the committee members themselves did not have the authority to discharge bills to a vote, like their contemporaries in the U.S. Congress, where committees have autonomy and power?

Besides, if any committee chair in Albany went his or her own way, he or she was not likely to remain chair for very long, forfeiting the attendant perks and influence. He or she might even face unexpected obstacles to getting reelected to another Albany term. The chair's or ranking minority member's job was to take marching orders from his or her house leader, who often issued directions after conferring with lobbyists, favored members, and senior staff.

As legislators, we were known and often even appreciated by our constituents. But in Albany, we were required to go along in order to get along, get ahead, and of course—to mention the singular preoccupation of career Albany politicians—get reelected. It was really that simple, and I came to realize that as an elected participant, it had corrosive effects on my sense of duty and obligations, and on that of the entire governmental system and state.

To me, the undemocratic way in which the state governmental system operates was exemplified many times by the habit of the leaders of both houses to give bleary-eyed legislators an hour or two, in the wee hours of the morning or night, to digest phone-book-thick bills and budget amendments before having to vote on the items in a preordained way. Under the state constitution, we were supposed to get three days to consider legislation. The avoidance of that requirement often relied on the excessive, even routine use of the Governor's so-called message of necessity—requiring votes within twenty-four hours in emergency situations. Its abuse further underscored our powerlessness and hobbled the processes of collaboration, review, and public involvement and debate most Americans expect from their elected representatives at all levels.

We—and our constituents—made no particular difference to the structure or results of the deal worked out by the Big Three and their staffs. The Governor only too happily contributed to this state of affairs. Our comments were barely tolerated, and if any of us dissented too loudly or too often from the leadership position, we soon found it redounding to our political and financial detriment (as in committee assignments and stipends, and even district and election aid).

After I was first elected in early 1996, and once I had gotten over my awe at how physically grand and impressive the Capitol was, I encountered the huge amount of rust that exists in the gears of the democratic process as it is practiced year in and year out in Albany. In other words, I came face-to-face with business as usual.

New York, the Empire State, had once been a model for state legislators nationwide. But it didn't really have much democracy left to speak of when I got there. Obscured by its elaborate mock-Gothic housing, flowery rhetoric, and rigid rules, it ran a bit like a regime. Leadership collaboration with most legislators was rare. Powerful lobbyists had disproportionate access to and influence on one or more of the Big Three. Ultimately, the voters were left out of the loop. At the end of session there were more lobbyists present than senators.

Making matters worse, during my time in the Senate, Pataki, Silver, and Bruno barely got along with one another, though their parties in many ways operated symbiotically to ensure that neither lost control of their respective houses on any given Election Day. Governors, too, preferred it that way— the better to have an opposite party, and one of the houses, to blame for their own inaction, ethical lapses, patronage, and boondoggles, or simply when their policies went awry.

Consider just one time-honored Albany routine—the dispensing of so-called member items. This is the rich gravy train from which legislators are permitted to ladle out funds to community organizations, with at least the implicit understanding that the grateful recipients will, in return, vote for them.

While a minority Democrat in the Republican-led Senate might expect perhaps $100,000 to $200,000 a year in member items to distribute sometimes for some useful services such as free lunches for seniors, summer park concerts, children's sports, and veterans' assistance, the Senate Republicans sometimes received ten times more. This was particularly true if they were entering a reelection campaign where some interparty competition was believed to exist. It was just one of the ways that the house leaders, whether Silver or Bruno, ensured that incumbents almost never lost an election, thereby freezing out new blood, new energy, and new ideas.

Now, these grants, in and of themselves, can and several times do serve valid civic purposes. Nonprofit organizations rely on them to buy fire engines and ambulances for volunteer companies, replace broken playground equipment, and support groups serving the poor and elderly. None is ever evaluated in terms of need and success, however. And some are quite unnecessary and even ludicrous, as good government groups and newspapers have pointed out.

But the overriding political purpose of the member items guarantees that only the squeaky, most formidable wheels get lubricated and that the organizations that depend on the grants are as beholden to the Albany triumvirate as are the local elected leaders. Here, in a way, is the ward heeler system of Boss Tweed's Tammany Hall (the one memorable politicians such as Mayor Fiorello La Guardia helped vanquish), wrapped in some kind of progressive disguise.

Pitch in to reelect the hand that feeds you, and you just might get a turkey at Christmas in return. Go your own way, and you get thin porridge. Former New York Governor Mario Cuomo was right when he told me that many member items, perhaps most, are "awful" and constitute "a slush fund of hundreds of millions of dollars without any state evaluation."

To further show that member items are seen as political capital, the money is often cut off to worthy community recipients in the event their district's assembly member or senator informs his leadership that he intends to retire. Such notifications are typically made six or seven months before an election. The member item money is then transferred to election races in which the incumbent faces a potentially serious challenge, in order to help the incumbent. The politicization of member item money unconscionably leaves community groups in the outgoing legislator's district to fend without anticipated aid, and often enough they must cut staff and services to the public.

A lawmaker's plans to leave office are held close to the vest by the leadership, the better to thwart any potential rivals to their handpicked replacement candidates and ensure that the successor is beholden to them should he or she be successful on Election Day. But what happens to his or her member items?

The years before I decided to retire, I regularly received about $150,000 to distribute. The organizations benefiting from these member-item funds fully expected to see them renewed after the next election. But after I told the Democratic

Minority Leader of the Senate, David Paterson, of my plans to retire almost a year before actually doing so, the $150,000 was effectively removed from my district starting with the date of my retirement announcement and doled out instead to other senators for their upcoming election races. The worthwhile projects in my district that I funded with member items were left empty-handed—a Catholic youth organization, a Jewish mental health group, a Latino community and cultural organization, an African American education project, and a soup kitchen. People suffered. Vital programs were hurt. There were three exceptions to the cutoff, based on the Senate Minority Leader's decisions. Some of the more powerful local groups had complained, and $5,000, $10,000 or $15,000 apiece was offered to keep them quiet. Other complainers were ignored. One community leader was told to "look to the future and forget the past," he recounted to me. He got the message and made his organization's pitch, after the election, to my successor.

Member items, of course, are decided behind closed doors, too. Just try to get an accounting of member-item expenditures by the legislators and Governor. It is difficult, sometimes impossible. At times, you might as well be asking for nuclear secrets from the Pentagon. As former Democratic senator Franz Leichter of Manhattan told me—Leichter spent many of his years in Albany hunting down and questioning the state budget's many hidden caches—the grants are intentionally scattered throughout each year's budget with recipient legislators' names left unmentioned, obscuring who gets what, and why.

The member item phenomenon began in the early 1980s, according to a 1984 article in the *New York Times*, which mentioned that member items had increased by 33 percent in one year, reaching $40 million within a $36 billion budget. In mid-2006, the paper editorialized that "slush funds" had reached $1 billion, including member items, in a budget of $112 billion, and demanded the total be reduced.

Assemblyman Sandy Galef of Ossining is one of the few elected officials who, in her fourteen years in the Legislature, has refused to accept any member items because they are such a murky part of the state budget, they are distributed to community entities in a non-equitable manner, and their use represents tax dollars spent without public consent. An April 4, 2006, *New York Post* editorial rightly called this an example of "Albany's Pork." The *Post* went on: "Two hundred million bucks—that's the lump sum buried in New York state's fiscal 2007 budget for 'services and expenses, grants in aid, or for contracts.' In fact, it's for what Albany euphemistically refers to as 'member items.'"

Does so opaque an accounting system work for the benefit of the public? There's no real way of knowing for sure. But, like the *New York Times* and Mario Cuomo, I very much doubt it.

Many legislators, of course, not only meet on the floor of the chambers but also see one another at social gatherings. At one such event, a prominent philanthropist mentioned to me that Senator Bruno wanted to meet with me in his office.

Bruno is a loquacious, robust man with a thick, high raft of white hair. He raised and rode horses on his ranch in Rensselaer County. His party usually caters to business interests, mine to union interests (although the powerful health care workers union was a happy beneficiary for its 2002 support of a Pataki third term). Still, many who disagreed with him on political issues respected him.

This was in the spring of 2002, a redistricting year, and the conversation quickly turned from pleasantries to his party's efforts to gain a Senate seat in New York City during that year's November elections.

He explained that his staff was in the process of redrawing the boundaries of several city districts to put pressure on Democrats, under what amounts to the legal gerrymandering that occurs every ten years in response to shifts in population tracked by the U.S. Census Bureau. It's a process that is supposed to ensure that minorities' voting rights are not diminished by demographic changes. For Bruno, I felt, the goal was to strengthen the precarious Republican majority in the Senate at any cost by redrawing districts to better suit that end.

Like so much else in Albany, the reapportionment process is misused. In Brooklyn, Bruno sought to create a new Republican seat, especially since he realized he probably couldn't maintain control of former Republican senator Roy Goodman's seat in Manhattan, the one that Liz Krueger, an independently wealthy liberal who had spent years directing a distinguished hunger-fighting organization, ultimately filled in a special election in early 2003 after Goodman's retirement.

"You're a reputable guy," Bruno told me, showing me a copy of a Brooklyn redistricting map, which didn't include my name in my own district yet included the name of a nominally Democratic councilman who planned to run for the Legislature that fall (though, in the end, unsuccessfully). "We'll give you the safest Democratic seat in Brooklyn." He also suggested that an additional "two to three million dollars" in member items would come my way if I switched parties. All you have to do is either become a Republican or do what we tell you to do, such as supporting me as Majority Leader, he said.

I was speechless in response, which isn't like me.

Soon Governor Pataki was part of the discussion. He called, and Bruno put him on the speakerphone.

"We'd love to have you in the Republican Party," the Governor intoned after exchanging pleasantries with Bruno and me. Bruno chatted with the Governor some more. When Bruno hung up the speakerphone, I sat there, staring at the Majority Leader and feeling disconcerted. I recovered soon enough. *No deal*, I thought.

"I have always been a Democrat and will remain a Democrat," I told the Majority Leader. And I walked out.

What happened in that meeting and in that election year in my small portion of the state was interesting for what it said about the gamesmanship that characterizes Albany. My largely white, Italian American, black, Latino, and Jewish Brooklyn base of voters, where I was a fairly popular figure due to years of constituent work with the help of an estimable staff, was cut into several areas by Bruno. One of the largest Jewish communities in the country became part of four (some critics said five) districts instead of the one I had represented—a dilution that was a blow to its political clout. It remained in the Borough Park, Coney Island, and Bensonhurst areas of Brooklyn and was additionally shoehorned into an entirely new swath within the north shore of Staten Island, across the Verrazano-Narrows Bridge. Sunset Park was substituted for Windsor Terrace and Brighton was taken out of the district entirely.

If ever I had entertained the thought of not running for re-election—and in truth, by then I had, because I was weary of such shenanigans, though I'd told no one but my wife, Susan—the Bruno face-off made me more determined than ever to run again and to win. I did win in the new district, by a 64 percent margin over my Republican opponent, Al Curtis, a former commissioner in then-mayor Rudolph Giuliani's highly centralized GOP administration at City Hall.

Bruno's gerrymandering, as engineered in consultation with him by his adviser, Steve Boggess, did succeed in achieving one of its main goals—to dislodge Brooklyn–Staten Island Democratic senator Vincent Gentile, who decided to run in the new "made for a Republican" district. For an incumbent legislator to lose an election is, as I've said, almost unheard of. But because of the kind of obstacles Gentile faced, aside from the new district boundaries drawn to favor his Republican opponent, Martin Golden, Gentile was unable to secure the support even of the influential Federation of Italian American Organizations, whose assistance he had enjoyed in past elections. He also witnessed a fellow Democrat, Brooklyn state senator Carl Kruger, campaigning for the Republican almost day and night (and without precedent) in return for new district boundaries that all but ensured his reelection for the next decade.

The problem was that Golden, an Irish American Republican, could offer the Federation of Italian American Organizations about $2 million in government funds for the construction of a youth center, courtesy of Bruno and his leverage over the state budget. Gentile, an Italian American Democrat, and Martin Connor, the Minority Leader of the Republican-led Senate, could not provide that kind of money.

The power of political leaders to determine the outcome of legislative elections hit me with new force in that election year. It's one thing to discuss the theory and history of a political body's democratic—small *d*—processes. It's quite another thing to be personally involved in the sordid reality. I knew then that this was about all I could take, and wouldn't run again.

After my reelection, given that my new district was cut into geographically and ethnically disparate areas, I approached the secretary of the Senate, the Bruno appointee Steve Boggess. As Bruno's point man, Boggess was a power to be reckoned with in many areas, from redistricting to office space. I asked him about the possibility of opening a second constituent services office on Staten Island. (The first district office in the state was opened in 1963 by liberal Manhattan legislators, paid for entirely with their own private funds. Within a few years, state funds were used to pay for any and all district constituent offices.)

But Boggess told me flatly, not once but twice, that under the rules of the Senate no senator was allowed public funding for more than one constituent office.

I was surprised, but I accepted his statement and paid what amounted to about $30,000 that year out of my own pocket to continue my Brooklyn office, while the state paid for my new Staten Island office, an essential beachhead to introduce myself to a new constituency and help resolve community and individual problems. Constituent service, after all, is the core of what any hardworking state representative worth his or her salt does. But then, surprise: a year and a half later a member of my staff discovered in the recesses of the budget that a dozen Republican senators, from various districts in New York City, Long Island, and upstate, each had two offices—paid for in full by the state government, and even those whose districts covered less terrain than mine.

So much about Albany breeds cynicism, so much of it stinks—the closed-door meetings, lobbyists insisting on quid pro quo, and vast amounts of questionable spending obscured by secrecy and sleight of hand.

I soon went to Paterson, by then the Minority Leader of the Senate, and asked for his advice, saying I wanted to go public to expose the special arrangements and the misinformation. These were just one of the countless ways in which Bruno rewarded loyalty with public funds. (A more common way was to give committee chairs special stipends of as much as $45,000 a year to those who did his bidding on committees and on the floor of the Senate.)

Paterson indicated he was surprised to discover that about a dozen Republicans were being allocated two offices—which were denied to me, a Democrat who was told that it was in violation of Senate rules to have two distinct offices. But just as quickly he urged me not to talk to the press about Boggess because it could have the unintended effect of reminding voters of the far deeper financial reserves that the state's Senate Republicans enjoy. The episode, if publicized, could diminish and weaken the Democrats by comparison.

I reluctantly went along, but wondered if there might be other reasons for asking me to bite my tongue. Assembly Speaker Silver had many special arrangements of his own with Democratic legislators, and he didn't want to open up an embarrassing shooting war with the Republicans on the subject. It all reminded me of the tacit understanding that existed between Bruno and Silver. *Leave us our majority in the Assembly,* goes the Democrats' unstated credo, *and we won't mess with you or yours in the Senate.* This is Albany's status quo, fortified against serious change from within or without.

Few New Yorkers who spend time inside Albany's insulated world—other than the politicians, their staffs, and the legion of lawyers, lobbyists, and consultants—recognize that state government is essentially a renewable wellspring of virtual permanent employment and revenue for its beneficiaries. Nor can they fully appreciate how much is at stake in how the place is run.

The truth is that Albany has at least as much influence over people's everyday lives and communities as the federal government.

Before the 1960s, some U.S. Supreme Court rulings went unheeded in the name of protecting states' rights in many parts of the North and South. The perception that gradually arose, as Americans watched on their black-and-white television screens while National Guard and Army troops moved in to enforce desegregation orders, was that many statehouses were corrupt and backward cesspools run by networks of white men beholden to the status quo.

Fast-forward to Ronald Reagan's presidency. Reagan invested new faith in the value of the states to spend taxpayers' dollars more sensibly than Washington did, to take over federal responsibilities—a trend that had further expression during the Clinton years, when, for example, the federal entitlement to welfare based on income was ended, and the states were permitted to fashion their own rules for giving out—or, as was often the case, withholding—welfare checks.

Even before the revived trend toward federalism, or dispersing powers of the national government (and, arguably, destabilizing and diminishing its ability to respond to national problems such as Hurricane Katrina in 2005), the states have long had clout over fundamental aspects in the lives of their citizens. Washington and of course New York City's city hall may get far more media attention, but the Governor and Legislature directly or indirectly determine such things as how effectively billions in Medicaid funds are used, where highways are built, when and which infrastructure repairs are made and by which companies or state agencies, how high the bridge and road tolls and bus and subway fares and assorted fees may go, and the extent and condition of the state's parks, forests, and

beaches. Taxes of every imaginable stripe, public college tuition rates and tuition breaks, the quality of school and college
physical plants, civil servants' pensions and experience requirements, licensing, private employees' pensions and wage
floors, economic development subsidies, hospital and housing
construction, small and large business grants, the quality of
the air we breathe and the water we drink—the list of how
much the state affects every one of its citizens goes on and on.

To consider Albany's influence and its current $112 billion
budget, and implicitly those of its troika, is enough to take
one's breath away. But trying to appreciate how many of its activities touching the public interest are conducted behind
closed doors by three men in a room is mind-boggling.

"Albany," wrote Eric Lane in the conservative *City Journal*
in the spring of 1997, "is anything but democratic."

Lane's prescient piece was a red flag in the long journey toward the day when, I hope, wholesale reform comes to Albany.

"Yes," he wrote, "New Yorkers cast their votes for State Assembly and Senate. When the vast majority of their representatives arrive at the Capitol, they don't legislate; they meekly
follow the instructions of their legislative leaders."

Lane, a Hofstra University School of Law professor, was
counsel to the minority Democrats in the State Senate from
1981 to 1986. He participated, he writes, in this "undemocratic
leadership culture and supported it." But after that experience,
which, as it did with me, spurred him to read extensively on
the principles of good lawmaking, he realized he had been on
the wrong path, and the Legislature's practices flouted nearly
every rule in the book of sound democratic governance—"an
embarrassing throwback to the days of bossism and party machines." In his article, he goes through a litany of problems
that characterized the Legislature and continues to this day,

even despite the spate of modest 2005 reforms born of secret negotiations by the Big Three after public pressure to clean up a rotten and broken system.

How many citizens know that during the legislative session, the workweek of the 212 legislators in the Capitol usually extends only to Wednesday, giving them time to beat the weekend rush out of Albany? This is true for the months of January, February, March, April, and May. In January they took a two-day week. June is a four-day week. Legislators in 2004 showed up just sixty-seven days in session in Albany, for which they received full-time pay (plus special stipends of a few hundred dollars each day they appeared in the chamber, if only for fifteen minutes or so, as was often the case). The rest of the time, many moonlighted as attorneys, real estate brokers, or insurance executives.

What goes on in the legislative chambers when they are there is carefully regulated by the ultimate paymasters—the leaders of both houses.

"In Congress . . . ," noted Lane, "members often engage in robust debate off the floor, especially on controversial measures. Members of both parties freely offer and adopt amendments, and it is difficult at times to predict how a bill will fare in a final vote, despite the best efforts of party leaders to ensure a certain outcome. By comparison, the New York State legislature looks like a meeting of the Supreme Soviet."

When a leader sends a bill to the floor, legislators understand it is their job to pass it as is, without amendment or comment, and not a single bill goes down to defeat on the floor unless guided by the leader's unmistakable hand. On July 11, 1996, in the last days of the session, the Legislature printed a 541-page, $18 billion bill covering Medicaid, mental health, and prisons—and passed it the very next day. It printed a 463-

page, $12 billion bill covering education and labor matters, and
passed it on the same day. It printed Governor Pataki's 53-page,
$1.75 billion Environmental Bond Act on July 12, and passed it
on the thirteenth.

As one might expect, party conferences are also firmly controlled. The weekly conferences are supposedly where legislators of the same political party get to make their voices heard
on bills, to weigh in on their potential impact, to discuss legislation from every vantage point. It is a time where, in theory,
legislative leaders listen to the arguments of their members,
lest they find themselves one day being voted out of their leadership posts by these same members, just as Ralph Marino was
ousted in 1995 and replaced by Bruno.

When one compares the Democratic conference meetings of
onetime Democratic Senate Minority Leader Martin Connor
with those run by his successor, David Paterson, one notices
differences as well as similarities. For example, Connor was basically a one-man show when he knew what he wanted, which
was most of the time. Even his second in command, Paterson
at the time, seldom was given an opportunity to influence Connor on major issues. Paterson's subsequent rise to take Connor's
place in the Senate arose partly from Democratic senators'
feeling of being cut out of the decision-making process. Under
Connor, there was little or no collaboration within the party on
many issues of importance.

Since seizing Connor's leadership position from him in
2002, Paterson has developed a different style. Paterson allows
the three or four top Senate Democratic leaders to work out positions on issues with him before anything is taken to a Democratic policy conference meeting. Paterson will often agree to
meet one-on-one with Democratic senators, unlike Connor,

but almost invariably after he and his top associates have already made up their minds. He doesn't even attend some conference meetings (though he goes more than Connor did), where, supposedly, stands on major issues are thrashed out. Under him, the conference leadership of three or four senators speaks in one voice. On occasion, differences do emerge, but rarely if ever on substantive matters. In 2006, the Democratic gubernatorial candidate, Eliot Spitzer, tapped the intelligent and articulate Paterson to be his running mate for lieutenant governor in the state election of that year.

Albany's self-serving and self-defeating tendencies remained so entrenched that the Brennan Center for Justice at New York University's School of Law published a truly devastating critique in 2004, minutely comparing the New York State Legislature to statehouses in the rest of the country. The media picked up on a catchphrase in a press release accompanying the report that aptly characterized Albany as "the most dysfunctional legislature in the country."

Well, maybe not the most. A case could be made that New York's is not the most dysfunctional capital of all.

But it comes close.

"New York's legislative process is broken," the Brennan Center study observed. A major point of the report dealt with the absence of a real committee system. In most modern legislatures, and certainly in Congress, committees are the center of legislative action. But not in New York. "Committees," the study reported, "have two principal functions: first, to enable legislators to develop, examine, solicit public and expert feedback, and improve bills in a specific area of expertise, and to convey the results of their work to the full chamber; and second, to oversee certain administrative agencies to ensure that they fulfill their statutory mandates. New York's committee system does not serve either of these functions."

There was as much concentration of leadership control during my tenure as ever in the Senate's and Assembly's history. It was fueled by the leaders' ample staffs, their unyielding grip on the powerful Rules Committee (which controls the flow of legislation to the floor), committee assignments, connections to certain lobbyists, deep and unaccountable reserves of political party funds, and influence over government hiring decisions, among many other levers of power and authority. Eleventh-hour efforts to reform the system after I left the Senate never redressed this fundamental imbalance, and never got to the deep-seated hurdles to representative democracy and resistance to change.

"They—the Big Three—have almost complete power," commented Manfred Ohrenstein, a former Minority Leader for Democrats in the State Senate. He was a senator from 1961 to 1994 and is now working as a lawyer in a growing firm. His comment rings as true as ever.

The Brennan report, for its part, found that less than one-half of 1 percent of the major bills passed by the Assembly and 0.7 percent of the major bills passed by the Senate—from 1997 through 2001—were the subject of a public hearing. This is unacceptable by any standard, except that of authoritarian systems of governance.

What is more, the report found that only 1.1 percent of the major bills passed by the Assembly and none of those adopted by the Senate during that same 1997–2001 period were the subject of committee reports, which are used in most legislative bodies to provide perspective, expertise, and analysis prior to a vote. That's stunning even to me. The New York State Sen-

ate had more standing committees—thirty-two of them—
than all but one other state chamber (the Mississippi State Senate, with thirty-five).

Somehow, the Brennan Center commentary that "the overall inactivity of committees in New York . . . renders this problem less acute than it would otherwise be" is not reassuring,
nor should it be. The study underlines that an anemic and cen-
trally controlled committee system prevents the Legislature in
Albany from cultivating bills in a manner that allows for collaboration, expertise, hearings, and committee reports on the
strengths and weaknesses of a proposal.

Legislators needn't even show up for committee votes, the
report emphasizes. Under the policy called empty-seat voting,
it also emphasizes, their absence was rigged to indicate prefer-
ence for the leadership's position. Who loses in this system? I
and some of my elected colleagues often asked ourselves during my tenure. The public. Who wins? Three men in a room—
the Senate Majority Leader, Assembly Speaker, and Governor,
who jostle, feud, and work out deals among themselves and
spring them on the public at the very last minute. When the
leaders aren't getting along, or can't see eye to eye—which is
common—the result is delay.

Some of the Brennan Center's other findings are also
alarming.

"Even when a bill has the support of a majority of legislators within a chamber," the report noted, "New York's Legislature makes it more difficult than any other legislature in the
country to discharge a bill from a committee for the full chamber to consider."

Albany also allowed the Senate Majority Leader and the Assembly Speaker "complete control" over the legislative calen-
dars to determine when and whether a bill that has been

reported out of a committee will be considered by the full Senate or Assembly.

In the past, for example, Bruno could suspend action on any bill listed on the Senate calendar by requesting that a star be placed beside its listing. No action could be taken until one day after the star, or a similar indicator, is removed. Does any other legislative chamber in the country give the Majority Leader such carte blanche over legislation? The answer, the report noted, is no.

New York legislators, in fact, introduced more bills than those in any other statehouse in the nation—a veritable cornucopia of legislation. A sign of productivity? Hardly. The lion's share of it was just for show. In 2002 alone, 16,892 bills were introduced in New York. Illinois, the next closest, had 8,717 and Massachusetts 7,924. One would think Albany was a beehive of activity. Yet precious few bills go anywhere except into press releases and publicly funded brochures sent to constituents.

From 1997 through 2001, the Senate voted on 7,109 bills, and the Assembly voted on 4,365 bills, according to the report. And more: those that made it to the floor of either chamber were in every instance approved, no exceptions, reflecting the near-absolute control of the leadership. Individual legislators, and thus their constituents, have virtually no direct way of obtaining votes on legislation they consider important without the approval of either of the house leaders.

Warren Anderson, a Republican who represented Binghamton in the Senate from 1966 to 1992 and was for many years that body's Majority Leader, told me that for much of his tenure legislators had more power through the committee system that existed at the time than they do now. "The average member has lost his independence," he said. "The power no longer resides in the chairman of the committee or the members of the Legislature. The power resides in the hands of the top leaders and their immediate staffs."

He added that the focus of Albany had shifted by the early 1990s to political survival. So it has remained.

"People only thought of survival, only thought of reelection, and only thought of safe seats," he said. "There were no real programs created in health or mental health or education or the arts originating with the members of the Legislature."

Anderson noted that while the Senate Majority Leader often had to at least consider, and will sometimes negotiate, the potential impact a bill will have on legislators from disparate parts of the state—those from industrial cities such as Buffalo, rural areas of the Adirondacks, or the suburbs of Long Island—the Speaker of the Assembly is even less challenged to negotiate with that house's legislators. That is because no single delegation group within the much larger Assembly, such as the Black and Latino Caucus, had enough votes to overturn the Speaker. "Bruno actually negotiates with his members, though he has procedurally taken their power away," said Anderson, who also praised Speaker Stanley Fink, the Brooklyn Democrat who led the Assembly while Anderson served as Senate Majority Leader.

There are, all the same, some observers who contend that if you want to effect wholesale reform in Albany, you merely work to change the leaders at election time. In other words, throw the "ins" out—in particular the Governor.

However, I would argue that whoever is in charge, and whatever the Legislature's rules or procedures, the house leaders and Governor will find a way to exert control over the decision-making process—as surely as water flows downhill—until and when the rules are drastically changed.

Opponents of the sweeping changes demanded by reformers contend that Albany has always been a battleground among conflicting interests, and always will be. Everyone recognizes that the competition for government contracts, regulatory favors, and laws has grown sharper thanks to a growing array of enormously well-funded and sophisticated lobbyists, consultants, party organizations, and political action committees—that is, special interests. It will always be so, they insist, no matter what.

I believe instead that not only must the public know who is pulling the strings and why, but also power in the Legislature must be diffused in a manner more consistent with the workings of the U.S. Congress. The Albany leaders have to be divested of their virtually absolute power, something that can be forced to happen only through public outrage and a constitutional convention. The Brennan report called for the leaders to change their own rules, and the result was largely cosmetic; the power dynamic remained intact despite the report's scathing findings. The same, I believe, would be the case under a new Governor from either party, and no matter which party controlled either or both of the legislative houses.

Every new day since the Brennan Center study brings reminders of Albany's dysfunction, not the reforms that are so desperately needed. In the early summer of 2005, the *New York Times* reported that a bill popular among consumer groups to make it easier to lease a car in New York had been killed through the efforts of Assembly Speaker Sheldon Silver.

Put aside the fact that trial lawyers, a powerful lobby in the State Capitol, have long opposed the change, and also that Silver is himself a trial lawyer. The key point is that a bill that looked like it might pass in the Assembly Transportation Committee in the summer of 2005 was not even permitted to come up for a vote. The committee chair, naturally a Silver appointee, suddenly took it off the agenda.

One member of the panel, a freshman legislator who had said he was leaning toward supporting the measure, explained that he had a change of heart, telling *Times* reporter Al Baker that he could see good points on both sides. A longtime Long Island legislator who had co-sponsored the bill was reassigned from the committee after Silver offered him a seat on a more desirable panel.

The upshot: the legislators left Albany, leaving unaltered an unpopular law that makes it relatively difficult to lease a car in the state. As it turned out, Congress later passed federal legislation making it easier for motorists in all states, including New York, to rent vehicles. The federal law effectively superseded Silver's resistance to change.

Silver's efforts favoring a special interest are hardly an isolated example. Baker, who writes from the *Times*'s Albany bureau, reported that at about the same time another popular bill suffered a similar roadblock at the behest of Senate Majority Leader Bruno, a measure pushed by lawmakers in the upper house for about a year to seal off a loophole that environmentalists contend has left numerous small, far-flung wetlands susceptible to development.

This measure had the backing of both Assembly Democrats and the Republican Governor. But Bruno repeatedly blocked it, calling it a needless burden on businesses and the sluggish upstate economy.

Whether it's the Democratic Assembly or the Republican Senate, the will of the lawmakers and, in effect, their constituents must take a backseat to the electoral concerns of their top leaders.

Still, there have always been rebels, such as former assemblyman Frank Barbaro of Brooklyn. He had numerous battles with the Speaker on the floor of the Assembly. But people such as Barbaro don't rise too far. (In Barbaro's case, his chairmanship of the labor committee didn't last, and he was eased out at the age of sixty-nine into a party-controlled New York State Supreme Court judgeship, from which he has since retired.) Nevertheless, it hardly takes a well-earned public fit of pique over the maddeningly top-down style of the Legislature's leaders to become known as something of a nuisance or threat.

When legislators can influence legislation, it is almost invariably through indirect means and outside the normal boundaries of choreographed conduct—and even then, nothing can become law without the leader's say-so.

Hate crime legislation was introduced by Senator Paterson more than a decade before it became law in 2000, after I joined the Senate and with the help of Senator Tom Duane and myself. As passed, after a long fight, it stiffened the penalties for crimes motivated by prejudice against a victim's race, religion, gender, or sexual orientation. Bruno's opposition was the reason it took so long to be adopted by the Legislature, more than forty years since the victories of the civil rights era.

During the struggle to get the bill passed, the Senate minority party established a task force on hate crimes legislation, and at one point we wanted to have a public hearing on the issue on Long Island to put pressure on Bruno.

It was easier said than done, because Nassau and Suffolk counties were considered Republican turf by the Senate leadership at the time, and not even Democratic leaders on Long Island were eager to provide a venue in their districts for the task force hearing for fear of angering Bruno.

A search for a public venue lasted for weeks, but Democrats were finally able to secure a meeting room at the city hall of

Long Beach, one of two Nassau County Democratic beach-heads (the other is Glen Cove). Then the Long Beach city hall reversed its position and turned us down. Such was the power on Long Island of the Senate Majority Leader and the local state senator, Dean Skelos, the Deputy Majority Leader of the Senate. Every senator from Long Island was a Republican, and Bruno and Skelos could make life difficult for them—and for Long Island Democrats in the Assembly as well, who needed cooperation across the aisle to get their bills passed. After Skelos informed the Long Beach Democratic assemblyman of our meeting, the assemblyman demanded that our approval be revoked and even protested to the Speaker.

The task force, with my help, scrambled to hold the public hearing in a Long Beach synagogue's meeting room. Happily, the hearing had the intended effect, drawing attention, via *Newsday* and other media outlets, to Bruno's opposition to hate crime penalties favored by many groups of voters—African Americans, Latinos, Jews, women, gays, liberals, crime victims' advocates, and all manner of civil rights organizations.

Not surprisingly, Skelos, the powerful Republican senator, was none too pleased by the temple meeting. He told me so when we bumped into each other at a reception later. He warned me to keep the issue out of Long Island in the future. I pointed out that Long Beach was a Democratic stronghold, but in reality it hardly mattered, because the Democratic assemblyman in Long Beach could not afford to alienate Skelos, unless he never again wished to see his name on a significant piece of legislation in Albany.

Nothing else happened with regard to hate crimes legislation until thousands of flyers were handed out by human rights groups at Long Island Rail Road stations. The media viewed the legislation favorably as the November 2000 elec-

tions approached. Both *Newsday* and the Long Island chapter
of the Anti-Defamation League called for a hate crimes law.

The Republicans, no fools, came on board, seeing little
advantage any longer in continuing Bruno's opposition to
making bias crimes a special category under the penal code.
Suddenly, the bill had new Republican champions in the Senate; they attached their names to it and, of course, with Bruno's
okay, nudged off the names of people such as myself. That was
fine with me. We took our names off and the Republicans put
their names on—this is how it's done in Albany. The bill's success was made possible for all the usual reasons, that is, the pur-
suit and protection of legislative seats rather than because of
any notion of justice for crime victims or prevention of harm
to any one group. But that, too, is how it works in Albany.

So it was with an education tax credit bill I had been working on since 1997, designed to help parents get a tax break on
the cost of a public or private educational institution attended
by their children. In 2001 it looked as if it had a good chance of
passing, but only with a different set of sponsors and in modified form. Even then it stalled and finally faded, even though
public schools would gain more than private schools, because
the education employee unions saw it—incorrectly—as a Tro-
jan horse for the conservative cause of tuition vouchers or
stipends for those eschewing public schools for private acade-
mies.

And so it also went with a bill to require insurance companies, a Republican constituency, to cover infertility drugs.
Democrats supported the measure, as they had in the past. I was
a co-sponsor; it was strongly supported by the American Infertility Association and by many of my Orthodox Jewish constituents. The bill was also potentially beneficial to countless
couples turning in record numbers to expensive infertility doc-

tors in order to have children. The Senate, gauging the cost to the big insurance companies and mindful of concerns of the Roman Catholic Church, consistently balked. It was not until an election year, 2002, that Republicans took it up, working out a compromise with the Assembly because they feared that their opposition to the measure could hurt them in some districts.

Naturally, my co-sponsorship was removed from the Senate's bill in the end because only Republicans could typically be listed on measures arising from the Senate.

Earlier in 2002, the Senate, in characteristic fashion, had tried to pass a version the leadership knew would not survive in the Assembly. It included clauses that would curb the cost and effectiveness of the insurance coverage provisions. The Republicans, it seemed, merely wanted to be able to issue a press release stating that they did something, when in fact their one-house bill would have done nothing. And indeed, nothing happened for five years, when additional negotiation and lobbying finally led to the passage of a bill that both houses' leaders could live with.

By the time I left office on December 31, 2004, I was disillusioned and fed up. I don't think some of my colleagues knew what to make of someone who insisted on considering the merits of an issue in addition to its political consequences. For instance, in 2005, when the state government passed its first on-time budget in two decades, it probably happened only because of the widespread criticism in newspapers across the state excoriating the Legislature's paralysis and ineptitude. It also occurred only after an election in which the politicians finally recognized that more and more voters were also fed up. But in no way did the first on-time enactment of the baroque, politically charged spending-and-revenue blueprint open the door to serious changes in how Albany works. Attorney Gen-

eral Eliot Spitzer called it an incomplete budget, and former
Governor Cuomo said it wasn't even a real one.

Nor did it compensate for the Legislature's customary failure to address many important issues of governance, not least
among them a ruling from the state's highest court to increase
state aid to New York City public schools by billions of dollars
to ensure a "sound, basic education," a requirement found in
the state constitution. Pataki had appealed the decision. Now
the Governor shrugged off the court's ruling, evoking, for me,
the widespread resistance of Southern states during the 1950s
and 1960s to court-ordered school desegregation. Pataki just
wanted the whole thing to go away until he departed from
office.

CHAPTER 3

The Governor Versus the Legislature

Clashes between big personalities, divergent upstate and downstate interests, organized economic forces, and rival political parties—all have been a constant in the history of New York State government. Governors have often loathed legislative leaders, and vice versa. Rivalries have been unforgiving at times. Greed and corruption, with more than a pinch of ambition for wealth and for power on a national scale, produced catalyzing scandals and, on occasion, lasting public consequences.

In New York's storied political history, secretive deals in smoke-filled rooms, framed by consideration of whatever collection of moneyed interests the top elected officials chose to serve, have been common. Cash has been the critical lubricant: receiving and dispensing it (in sealed brown envelopes or through legal, albeit loosely supervised, campaign channels) has been the abiding preoccupation, which is to say the prevailing concern is political survival and aggrandizement rather than principle. From its beginnings, Albany, for all its lofty rhetoric and even loftier architectural setting, has never been a magnet for piety, propriety, and good works.

Nevertheless, out of the cauldron of expedient conduct and

craven behavior has come some of the most progressive and humane legislation passed by any state at any time. Unfortunately, you usually have to look back many decades to find it.

The history of New York State is endowed with legendary and often stormy personalities who have occupied the Governor's mansion, among them DeWitt Clinton, Al Smith, Franklin Roosevelt, Herbert Lehman, Thomas Dewey, and Nelson Rockefeller.

In more recent times, Hugh Carey risked his political future by helping pull New York City and New York State back from the brink of bankruptcy, a monumental rescue, and Mario Cuomo, liberal lion of his generation and a moving orator, succeeded in imposing some of the first significant ethical standards on the legislative and executive branches.

Cuomo and Carey are also remembered for standing fast against legislators and a majority of voters who were demanding the death penalty, while vastly enlarging the state's correctional capacity (and thus increasing prison-based employment in recession-battered upstate regions). George Pataki defeated the three-term Cuomo in the 1994 gubernatorial election in part on a platform embracing capital punishment, though no one on death row was given a lethal injection during Pataki's dozen years in office.

In any case, strong Governors have been a feature of New York State government for generations. The Legislature's use of its constitutional power to override the Governor's veto has been exceedingly rare. Between 1870 and 1976, not a single gubernatorial veto was overridden by the Legislature, suggesting the power of the executive branch. However, more recently, especially under Governor Pataki, there has been an increase in the number of vetoes that have been overridden. Strong-willed executives fought back against occasionally defiant Legislatures, yielding no more than they were forced to, then compromising grudgingly to keep the veto streak intact.

During the latter half of the twentieth century and into the present day, state politics have become increasingly complex, with increasingly diverse and varied interests—consumer groups, labor unions, industries—using or vying with an unprecedented hired army of lobbyists and unparalleled amounts of campaign cash to gain access, legislation, regulatory relief, and funding. And there are grassroots activists, citizens groups, and nonprofit organizations of all stripes.

The common goal is to educate public opinion, but more important is applying pressure upon or wooing the two top leaders of the Legislature and the Governor. Like kings, these three sift the pressures weighing on them from within and without and—with little or no public debate—cut their political deals.

The Legislature, meanwhile, remains at its core what it has always been known to be: a self-perpetuating institution, offering virtually lifetime jobs for those legislators willing to play by the leaders' rules. The government is a huge generator of patronage for the party faithful, to such a degree that it would be difficult to imagine the struggling upstate economy being able to survive on its own if it were weaned from the public trough. This may be the state bureaucracy's biggest virtue, as an important hedge against the vicissitudes of the market economy for tens of thousands of New Yorkers, their families, and their towns.

Given that it is such an enormous money machine, there have been few serious, open debates about public policies affecting the citizenry. Absent an activist Governor and an aroused and informed public, the "Albany game"—going along to get along, and not making too many waves or problems for the leadership—rolls on. Hugh Carey, in a conversation with me, described his frustration with the "dark alliances" of most legislators, their fealty toward anyone who agrees to help them get reelected. Consequently, making policy on the merits is nearly impossible.

Since it was named the state capital in 1782, Albany has proved conveniently removed from the prying eyes of the nation's media capital, which even then was Manhattan. Situated within relatively easy reach of New York City, Montreal, and Boston, Albany, then with a population of 42,700, was the sixth-largest city in post-Revolutionary America. Its national importance as the capital of the "Empire State" was established firmly in 1825 with the opening of the Erie Canal, the epic public works feat championed by DeWitt Clinton that turned Albany into a significant inland seaport and New York City into an international crossroads of trade and commerce.

The great DeWitt Clinton, elected to the governorship in 1817, changed the nation in a dramatic fashion. Interestingly, he clashed with the Legislature and faced opposition from politicians and their conservative business supporters, who believed his relentless support of the Erie Canal project, which they derided as "Clinton's ditch," was nothing more than a boondoggle.

But the canal was built, and finally, in October 1825, Clinton arrived triumphantly in Manhattan to celebrate the grand opening of the waterway. The canal also made New York City a political and cultural force for the nation and triggered the westward movement of American settlers. The epic migration opened up vast tracts of rich farmland in the Northwest Territories, which would in time become Illinois, Indiana, Michigan, and Ohio, all of which had earlier been basically inaccessible to the large-scale movement of settlers and traders.

No subsequent Governor, except perhaps Al Smith, has ever approached Clinton for believing in and carrying out a transcendent vision that has transformed the nation and the state.

Some New York Governors became president. Grover Cleveland, who started public life as a Buffalo attorney, was a self-proclaimed reforming Governor between 1883 and 1885 (Governors then served two-year terms). A Democrat, he was saddled with a very conservative and even obstructionist Legislature, and in the end his brief gubernatorial record was less than memorable. He was, however, a smart enough politician to develop a working relationship with an energetic, reform-minded Republican assemblyman from Sagamore Hill in Long Island's Oyster Bay named Theodore Roosevelt.

Roosevelt was a man of urgency and ambition. President Benjamin Harrison, after his election in 1889, appointed Roosevelt as a member of the United States Civil Service Commission. He held the post until 1895, when he became New York City police commissioner, styling himself a reformer and combating police corruption. In 1897 he joined President William McKinley's administration as assistant secretary of the Navy, zealously preparing for the war in Cuba. When the Spanish-American War erupted in 1898, he left and became lieutenant colonel of a regiment of volunteer cavalry he had organized from hunters and cowboys from the West, winning fame as leader of these Rough Riders in a charge up San Juan Hill against Spanish troops. He forever after reveled in the public's adulation of his warrior image. Roosevelt struck a responsive chord in those who believed the invasion was "a splendid little war," in Secretary of State John Hay's indelicate description.

"The charge itself was great fun," Roosevelt wrote his family from Cuba.

The press showed pictures of Roosevelt on horseback, striking a heroic pose, leading his foot soldiers up the hill. With TR's ego expanding by the day, the American satirist Finley Peter Dunne had Mr. Dooley, his fictional Irish immigrant, saying of Roosevelt's breathless memoir of the war, "If I was him, I'd call the book 'Alone in Cuba.' " William Graham Sumner, the Yale sociologist and social Darwinist, was an anti-imperialist who despised TR. He dismissed the widespread spirit of triumphalism and flag-waving, saying, "My patriotism is outraged by the notion that the United States never was a great nation until in a petty three-month campaign it knocked to pieces a poor, decrepit, bankrupt old state like Spain."

Roosevelt campaigned for New York Governor in 1898 as a war hero, evoking the supposed glories of San Juan Hill and extolling the nation's new imperialism in the Caribbean. He was elected by a small margin—"New York cares little for the war," Roosevelt lamented—and served as Governor from 1899 to 1901. But he soon found Albany somewhat too provincial for his agenda.

In Albany, he quickly found that conservative politicians were in agreement with his nationalistic appeals, but they didn't like it when he spoke loudly about reforming the corruption-riddled state government so that it might become more responsive to its citizens. They were especially unhappy about his unpredictability and independence of mind, which led Senator Thomas Platt, the state Republican Party boss, to want him pushed out of Albany at the earliest possible moment.

Ohio's Republican boss, Mark Hanna, was apoplectic when he heard the news that Governor Roosevelt might be chosen to be McKinley's vice president. "Don't any of you realize," he famously warned his fellow Republican convention delegates, "that there's only one life between this madman and the White House?"

Governor Roosevelt did push through environmental protections and streamlined civil service requirements, neither of which most conservative legislators had much sympathy for. When, after his single two-year term, he departed Albany to become McKinley's vice president, he unselfconsciously trumpeted, "I think I have been the best governor within my time, better than either Cleveland or [Samuel J.] Tilden"—a remark historian Henry Pringle termed "a shade overenthusiastic." Then, in eerie fulfillment of Hanna's fears, he assumed the presidency after William McKinley was assassinated in Buffalo in 1901.

Two quickly forgettable politicians succeeded the swashbuckling Roosevelt, until Charles Evans Hughes, an ambitious reformist politician, was elected Governor in 1906. Hughes fought hard for and won a state public service commission, as well as reforms of the insurance industry. He abruptly resigned when President William Howard Taft named him to the Supreme Court in 1910.

Six years later Hughes ran unsuccessfully for the presidency. He retired for the night after the polls closed in the East, believing he had beaten Woodrow Wilson. He awoke to learn that he hadn't because, while he slept, California had gone for Wilson.

A close second in influence to the Governors in any era are the leaders of the Assembly and Senate. The legislative branches preside in august and elegant chambers. The interior of the Senate, for example, is a luxuriant mix of ornate Greek and Roman styles. The overpowering sense of permanency and height found in both chambers symbolizes a legal power and authority over everyone living in the state. Some have said that the New York State chamber looks even more impressive than the United States Senate chamber.

Legislative leaders have enormous powers in modern times, the go-to guys in their respective houses. Historically, they have served as allies, rivals, or patsies to their Governors.

"Some pundits call the legislative leadership position 'the hardest job in Albany to get, and the easiest to keep,' " wrote Robert B. Ward in *New York State Government: What It Does, How It Works.* Ward also commented on a basic rule of Albany politics: "If the leadership in a given house wants a bill to pass, it will." The crucial question, he noted, is "how to get the Senate Majority Leader and the Assembly speaker to want a bill to pass."

The near-absolute authority of the leaders has been the modern norm, as counterweight to a strong executive branch. Occasionally, though, someone has been forced to abdicate, such as Republican Majority Leader Ralph Marino, who did so in 1994. It was because the newly elected Governor Pataki was reportedly upset that Marino had opposed his campaign for the Republican nomination the year before.

Throughout the state's history, the Legislature's leaders have been called upon to satisfy their loyal fellow party members by offering ever-larger perks, ranging from unaccountable member items to patronage jobs for their friends and larger Albany offices for members and staffs. That's for the majority party of a respective house. The minority gets the leavings.

Despite infrequent successes at reform over the course of state history, noted Queens assemblyman and future state comptroller Alan Hevesi in 1975 wrote, "even advocates of legislative reform often come out in favor of the kind of centralization of power and responsibility in the hands of party leaders." The central question rarely goes beyond an immediate, strategic determination of how far the leaders will choose to cooperate with the Governor, and whether they will rule their respective houses with a take-no-prisoners style or in a rarer, more collaborative style.

Alfred E. Smith, perhaps New York's greatest Governor of modern times, arrived in Albany in 1903 as an assemblyman during a period of enormous social change. Far more people lived in cities than on farms, where independent yeomen were being displaced by larger-scale commercial agriculture. Millionaires and gigantic trusts had emerged in the wake of the rapid industrialization of the late nineteenth century. Immigrants were still arriving from an impoverished Europe by the millions, many flocking to Smith's Lower East Side neighborhood.

Born in 1873 in a South Street tenement near the Brooklyn Bridge, the son of an Irish trucker fascinated by the political life, Smith was a consummate New York City ethnic politician, a self-appointed "man of the people." He was a liberal, his rasping voice that of a street-smart wisenheimer. He had a conquering, swaggering, proud-to-be-a-New-Yawkah stance.

Smith's autobiography, *Up to Now*, is among the finest ever written by a politician, "a plain story of a plain ordinary man written from memory," as he put it. The memoir recalled with nostalgia and reverence his Fourth Ward's party rallies and clubhouse speakers on lower Manhattan's crowded street corners, the gifts and favors handed out to immigrant newcomers by local ward heelers, the "honest" graft, the rousing Election Day celebrations, the good talk and fellowship in local saloons and Tammany clubhouses. One Tammany state senator, long since forgotten, is portrayed as "the greatest campaign orator and debater I ever heard."

In 1903, at age thirty and a product of the Tammany wigwam, Smith was elected to the State Assembly. Despite his political heritage, no one ever accused Smith of taking a dime that was not his own. He worked hard as an assemblyman, and while others were out cavorting in Albany's fleshpots—at that time the city had a number of flourishing houses of gambling and prostitution—he went home to read the bills and laws that few cared to digest. The knowledge and legislative sophistication he garnered led his colleagues to select him as their Majority Leader. His biographer Robert Slayton notes that his Tammany bosses soon saw to it that he was chosen chair of the Ways and Means Committee, where he was able to decide which proposed bills could or could not be considered by legislators.

At first, the inexperienced Smith was disappointed with the capital, less because of the city's sordid political environment, which probably reminded him of Tammany Hall, than because of the depressing physical condition of the city itself. He preferred to commute from Manhattan so that he could be with his wife and children and cherished pets, whose intelligence he once compared favorably to that of certain legislators. Many of those colleagues continued partying in the brothels and casinos, but Smith, ever the traditional Roman Catholic and exemplary family man, would have none of it.

Smith, a budding humanitarian, read some of the literature of the Progressive Era then sweeping the nation. More than likely he became familiar with its crusading journalistic accounts of injustices in field and factory, farms and cities, and slowly developed an affinity for workers struggling against corporate behemoths.

The Triangle Shirtwaist fire on March 25, 1911, which killed 146 workers, mainly girls and women, changed him as well as his ally on the Senate side, Robert Wagner. Wagner, the State Senate Majority Leader (later a prominent U.S. senator and New Dealer) and another loyal Tammany man with genuine reform impulses, was chosen as chair of the Legislature's Factory Investigating Commission in 1911. Smith, as Speaker of the Assembly, was its vice chairman.

Shepherded by Frances Perkins, the commission's main investigator, the two men discovered that aisles had been blocked and exits locked inside the factory. Meanwhile, the press published photos of terrified employees jumping to their death in an effort to escape the smoke and flames. There was an enormous outpouring of public outrage at the atrocious, Dickensian commercial firetraps proliferating throughout the city and state. The moment was Smith's (and Wagner's) epiphany, altering their view of what elected officials could do to relieve the burdens of the working poor. "In brief," wrote Smith, "it was the aim of the commission to devote itself to a consideration of measures that had for their purpose the conservation of life."

He learned to his horror that the state and the Legislature had done virtually nothing about any of the conditions that contributed to all of this. Inspections of workplaces were rare and announced in an advance. Children and pregnant women labored in firetraps. At one of the committee meetings in the Assembly, he heard that a well-connected cannery was employing women and young children for up to sixteen hours daily. Soon after, he successfully urged the Assembly to enact a law granting one rest day per week for all workers. The cannery firm and its legislative allies fought it, but Smith can best be remembered for having risen and intoned, "Remember the Sabbath Day, to keep it holy, but I am unable to find any language in it that says 'except in the canneries.' "

Smith became so possessed with changing things that he schooled his Tammany mentor, Charles Francis Murphy, a latter-day convert to economic and political reform. Murphy, perhaps the shrewdest and most flexible boss Tammany ever had, knew enough to understand that the machine could not stand in the way of serious change in the Legislature. Not that he signaled his intentions to any except his most loyal subordinates, Smith and Wagner. When asked why Mr. Murphy—he was always "Mr. Murphy" to Smith and others—failed to sing the national anthem when it was played, a Tammany card wisecracked, "Perhaps he doesn't want to commit himself." But he did, behind the scenes, making sure that frequently erupting scandals or accusations never tarred Smith and Wagner while encouraging them as they helped enact such laws as the Workmen's Compensation Act in 1911. There were many other reforms designed to ease the burden of working people—the common goal for Smith and the German-born Wagner—in addition to their desire to overhaul the state's administrative machinery.

Whatever the Tammany gang's prodigious role in dirty politics and good or bad corruption (as George Washington Plunkitt drew the distinction), Murphy's blessings provided Smith (and Wagner, too) full Democratic Party support when he became Governor, setting in motion the liberal and humanitarian laws that, in spite of continual and ferocious skirmishes with rural upstate and conservative politicians inside the Legislature as well as economic interests, would become the hallmark of Franklin Roosevelt's New Deal and Herbert Lehman's years as Governor of New York.

Along with the rising demands and economic power of the recent waves of immigrants, especially Jews, Italians, and Irish, came increasing communist and socialist demands and mass protests, as well as organized labor's insistence on the legal right to unionize. One can only compare Smith's legislative achievements in furthering unionism and the rights of economically oppressed masses with those of the famed Progressive Robert La Follette in Wisconsin. "The supreme issue, involving all the others," La Follette wrote in *La Follette's Autobiography* in 1913, "is the enrichment of the powerful few upon the rights of the many," a faith shared in the wake of the Progressive Era by Governors in Iowa, Kansas, Nebraska, Indiana, and Oregon and by Charles Evans Hughes. In New York, Al Smith absorbed that faith and was its prime mover.

Elected Governor in 1918, defeated in 1920 by Republican Nathan L. Miller, but returned to the statehouse in 1922, Smith went on to serve three additional terms. He became a master of Albany's legislative process and arcane ways.

In his magisterial biography of Smith protégé Robert Moses, *The Power Broker*, Robert A. Caro writes of the Bureau of Municipal Research's 768-page report, issued in 1915. Smith and everyone else could read in that detailed accounting of state government of the existence of 169 distinct agencies, departments, commissions, committees, and departments with swirling, spaghetti-like strands of accountability and authority, some leading to the Governor, some to the legislative bosses, and some to Lord knows who.

"The governor possessed little authority," Caro explained. "Not he, but the chairmen of the various committees of the reactionary and corrupt Legislature controlled the state's purse." Because power was essentially vested in the Legislature, reformers from 1915 on understood that "more than any other single fact, [it] explained the utter failure of 20 years of effort by a succession of liberal governors such as Roosevelt and Hughes to increase the involvement of the state with the new needs of the people."

Smith carried through the thoroughgoing reorganization of hundreds of largely unaccountable state agencies, which had acted as they wished without any control from Albany. The trick was to wrest power from what he deemed an obstructionist Legislature. Adapting the proposals of earlier reformers and the Bureau of Municipal Research study, he centralized the agencies (which in 1919 had grown to 187, his aide Robert Moses found) and allowed them only to make recommendations to the Governor, who had the option of forwarding those recommendations with his budget to the Legislature. Too, the Governor's term would be increased to four years.

By winning elections and through constitutional amendments, he established eighteen state departments. "It was," Warren Moscow, who covered Albany for the *New York Times* for many years, wrote in his 1948 book *Politics in the Empire State,* "the most thorough renovation of a state government the nation had ever seen until then."

Smith battled and won better conditions for working people, a form of workmen's compensation for injuries on the job, and restrictions on child labor. This son of Manhattan's streets was also an ardent conservationist. And he established some of the first low-cost housing projects in the country, the Amalgamated Clothing Workers Union project in the Bronx and another on the Lower East Side of Manhattan. He received legislative approval for equal pay for female public school teachers and persuaded the public to support bond issues on behalf of state hospitals and mental institutions. He even assigned Robert Moses to carry out a rehabilitation program for young prisoners. Smith's achievements were not always easily obtained from a largely conservative Legislature. But by threats to veto all Republican money bills, he was able to gain many of the measures he deemed vital.

True to his Progressivism, Smith was also a remarkably courageous and outspoken defender of civil liberties, not merely during tranquil years but also during the post–World War I era marred by the infamous Palmer Raids and Red Scare. When socialist politicians in Albany were threatened with expulsion as "enemies of the government" in 1919 by the Legislature's Lusk Committee, Smith excoriated the "false atmosphere" of vigilante justice and denounced the committee's action as "undemocratic" and "un-American." Unlike many politicians of the time, he challenged the expulsions. And when the Lusk Committee also chose to require loyalty oaths from public school teachers, he confronted supporters of the bill, calling them "hysterical and interested in the control of liberal thought," and promptly vetoed it. "The bill confers upon the Commissioner of Education a power of interference with freedom of opinion which strikes at the foundations of democratic education," he said.

After Smith left Albany following four terms as Governor, the great event in New York's political life was when he was chosen by the Democrats to run for the presidency against Republican Herbert Hoover in 1928. Franklin D. Roosevelt, the future Governor and president, delivered the nominating speech for the Democratic Party. It was the first time a major political party had ever nominated a Catholic. The shock of his campaign was not his defeat but rather the vicious anti-Catholicism that surfaced among so many voters across the nation.

Al Smith died on October 4, 1944. At his funeral in New

York City's St. Patrick's Cathedral, Frances Perkins remembered her old friend and colleague as "the man responsible for the first drift in the United States toward the conception that political responsibility involved a duty to improve the life of the people."

After Smith's reign, the Governor's office grew in power to match the stature and sweep it had derived in part from Smith's gale-force energy, style, and will. If there is a time and place in which the seeds for today's "three men in a room" were planted—the origins, that is, for the situation now in which legislators are handed budget bills hundreds of pages long to digest within two or three hours of voting, or can cast votes on legislation in keeping with their leaders' wishes without even being present in the chambers when the votes are counted—it is worthwhile to look at the ways that legislative leaders post-Smith sought to consolidate their influence to offset the executive branch. Warren Anderson, who was the Senate Majority Leader during Nelson Rockefeller's years in the Governor's mansion, said he never met alone with Rockefeller and the Assembly Speaker; both leaders also brought along the chairman of the committee whose issues were on the Governor's discussion agenda. "I didn't deal with only two people, and I would never deal with just the Governor alone," Anderson, an elder statesman now in his nineties, said in an interview for this book.

Still, starting in the 1970s, procedures appeared that increasingly institutionalized the power of the Assembly and Senate leaders over their minions—procedures that emphasized emergency action over slow deliberation in the wake of the disastrous New York City fiscal crisis of those years, which required emergency state legislation on an unusually fast track. In ensuing years, leaders also took greater and greater control of the workings of their political parties, deciding which legislator would face a primary and which one would have a free ride to reelection, for example, or who would receive prestigious committee assignments, see his or her name attached to important bills, or receive generous district aid as well as campaign funds in election years.

The decades of drift toward centralization had still other roots. Sheldon Silver, for example, enjoys a huge, unprecedented Democratic majority in the Assembly, a ratio of two Democrats for every Republican; Bruno's 35–27 Republican majority in the Senate is perilously puny by comparison. Both situations, as it happens, have militated against democratization in Albany, as Silver goes largely unchallenged and Bruno somewhat nervously holds on to the GOP reins.

In addition, the tendencies of the sitting Governors have also played a role in the way laws are enacted. When Thomas E. Dewey was Governor (1942–54), both houses were ruled by Republicans; he would call the two legislative leaders to his living room at times, where they'd discuss his agenda. Mario Cuomo, for other reasons, tried to exert his influence by consensus with the two top legislative leaders, one of them a Republican and the other a Democrat; it was easier than trying to appeal to the varied and conflicting voting segments within the Assembly and Senate. Thus evolved, over the course of a couple of generations, the escalating measure of control over New York State government held in the hands of the Governor and the Assembly and Senate leaders. But there are even older examples.

Franklin Roosevelt was asked to run for Governor following Al Smith's fourth and final term as Governor. He won the election by 25,000 votes out of 2.2 million cast. Starting with his first year in power, 1929, FDR battled the Legislature with his

pioneering use of radio talks that would later become a national phenomenon during his years in the White House. Sam
Rosenman, his ever-present friend and adviser and sometime
speechwriter (he helped compose FDR's initial major campaign speech in 1928), described how his boss proposed, in a
personal appearance before the Republican-dominated Legislature during the bleakest days of the Great Depression in
1931, that new taxes be enacted "to provide [poor and jobless
people] with food against starvation and with clothing and
shelter against suffering." His proposal infuriated conservative
lawmakers and business interests. "The very foundation of the
state is in danger from this message of avarice, usurpation and
presumption," shouted a Republican assemblyman about Roosevelt's proposals.

In time, the measure was passed because of FDR's political
wiles, as well as the devastating toll the Depression was exact-
ing throughout the state. Still, legislators fought back fero-
ciously. Vetoes and failed attempts to override followed
regularly. Exasperated and furious at being denied by the Legislature, Roosevelt told the press that in spite of Al Smith's
modernization of state machinery, nothing much had changed
since the time he had been in the Legislature.

When Roosevelt departed Albany for Washington in 1932,
the New Deal programs he would push through were built in
part on Smith's successes and philosophy. Indeed, FDR named
Frances Perkins as his secretary of labor, the nation's first female cabinet member. Moreover, FDR once said that the goal
of his administration was "to make a country in which no one
is left out." It can be argued that sentiment was straight out of
Smith, Wagner, and Perkins.

FDR's successor in Albany was a dedicated liberal, Herbert
Lehman. The historian Allan Nevins described working as a

reporter for the *New York World* in Albany in the preface to his 1963 book, *Herbert H. Lehman and His Era.*

"Each house was usually controlled by a small group of iron-fisted leaders who kept what was euphemistically called debate under tight control," Nevins recalled. Many of the members, he found, owed their seats to lobbies and special interests. "Altogether," he concluded, as others have before and since, "legislative Albany had its seamy aspect."

Like Smith and FDR, Lehman was perfectly happy to confront a Republican-dominated Legislature, since it could then be blamed for the state's problems. As a result, Lehman's relationship with the Legislature was, wrote Nevins, "one of the most turbulent in the annals of the state." In the 1935 session, for example, Assembly Speaker Irwin Steingut had to call in state troopers so that his loud and raucous members wouldn't quit the Assembly or cause a riot. The *New York Herald Tribune*, Republican and conservative in its editorial bent, gloated, "Legislature Ends in Row After 28 ½ Hour Tumult," and editorialized, "Nothing to Be Proud Of." Yet as Nevins, Lehman's sympathetic biographer, noted, a long list of badly needed reforms took place under Lehman's leadership, such as unemployment insurance, free milk for impoverished children, and raising the age at which children were permitted to quit school to sixteen. Despite opposition by the Legislature, Lehman won the right to have the state join thirty-three others that had chosen to join the nascent federal Social Security Act. As Governor he also forced the Legislature to enact a minimum wage for female employees, added some muscle to worker's compensation laws, and, shortly before leaving Albany, helped make public housing an accepted principle by forging a bipartisan agreement allowing the state to assume responsibility for low-income families seeking housing.

Though Lehman was too often deemed a plodder and a poor public speaker, his successes belied this image. At the Democratic convention nominating FDR for the presidency in 1932, Lehman raised the delegates to an emotional frenzy in defending FDR and the hopes of containing and overcoming the Great Depression.

Thomas E. Dewey, Lehman's successor, had been the crusading New York County district attorney. He prosecuted the likes of Waxey Gordon, Lucky Luciano, Lepke Buchalter, and Tammany boss Jimmy Hines. He arrived in Albany in 1943 a political moderate with libertarian sentiments. He placed his political faith in state and local government and much less in the federal government, in contrast to his predecessors. It was, he critically reasoned, a too-great reliance on the central government, a development magnified by the economic disaster of the 1930s and the coming of war.

"Life is more than unemployment, sickness and old age," he said. "Life is alive and vital, to be lived and enjoyed." By which he meant less power for the national government in Washington, fewer taxes, less waste in state government, and more reliance on a "vigorous and productive economic system."

During his tenure, the onetime small-town boy from Owosso, Michigan, established the foundations of an effective state university system (which would eventually lead to Nelson Rockefeller's creation of a sterling network of state-supported community colleges, four-year colleges, and four major universities), began a state thruway, and helped pass one of the first civil rights bills in the nation, the Ives-Quinn law, which effectively rendered racial discrimination in hiring illegal. As a result, one of the bill's supporters, Alvin Johnson, the first president of the New School for Social Research, called Dewey "a liberal without blinkers." Obviously pleased, Dewey applauded Johnson as a realistic visionary "willing to wait until Monday morning if the millennium can be sure of arriving and be a little better when it comes."

Overstaffing and party patronage in Albany's agencies and departments were commonplace. According to Richard Norton Smith, Dewey's biographer, Dewey learned it took twenty-nine office workers to order 70 cents' worth of glue. State employees in no-show jobs were fired. Resisting farm lobbyists, he shut down the Milk Publicity Board, "a $300,000-a-year nest of patronage jobs." And possibly because of his experience as a district attorney confronting organized crime, he had a tendency to act swiftly without seeking anyone's approval (including the Legislature's) where there were obvious injustices affecting the most vulnerable. As Richard Norton Smith described it, without waiting for lengthy commission hearings and copious studies, he reacted immediately when he heard from Republican state senator Seymour Halpern about dangerous and unbearable conditions Halpern had seen in Creedmoor Hospital, a mental institution housing 4,500 patients in his Queens district. Dewey followed up with a very brief inquiry, which concluded that Creedmoor was a "Bastille of despair," and ordered heads to roll and the state Mental Hygiene Department roundly censured.

Like most Governors, he and the Legislature were not the closest of allies; their relationship can best be described as contentious and combative. Again, like nearly all Governors, Dewey tried verbal persuasion, strong-arm tactics, trade-offs—and the veto. He turned down almost one-third of the bills passed in the Legislature.

During the last day of the legislative session in March 1944, he was appalled by an innocuous bill that had passed, dealing with teachers in the New York City schools. Applying every bit of pressure he could muster, Dewey forced the Assembly and Senate to scotch it. Outraged, Senate Majority Leader John J. Dunnigan denounced Dewey's legislative allies in both parties. Dunnigan berated his beaten and frazzled colleagues huddled in their seats: "Who runs this Legislature anyway, us or the Governor?" Victorious, Dewey smilingly called them "my Legislature."

Future Governors such as Nelson Rockefeller, Hugh Carey, and Mario Cuomo felt the same way, with Carey vetoing bill after bill that arose from the Legislature, sometimes just to put legislators in their place. Rockefeller, in particular, had little trouble keeping the Assembly and Senate in line. In 2005, former Governor Carey told me without too much exaggeration that Rockefeller, as Governor, "owned" his own political party outright and "leased" the other.

Dewey's successor, Averell Harriman, was the child of Edward Henry Harriman, the railroad tycoon. In 1954, Harriman, after a career in national and international politics—he was there when FDR and Winston Churchill drew up the Atlantic Charter in August 1941 and later served as U.S. ambassador to the Soviet Union and Great Britain and also as Harry Truman's secretary of commerce—chose to go to the state level. A Democrat, he beat Thomas Dewey's ally Irving M. Ives in the race to run New York State. Among Harriman's worthwhile contributions as Governor was trying to reform policy concerning the mentally ill. His administration sought to have local governments set up community-managed treatment sites, with the state paying half the cost.

Harriman, like Rockefeller, was born to great wealth, and the parallels didn't stop there (for example, each man unsuccessfully sought his party's nomination for the presidency). In 1957, speaking informally to reporters covering the Albany beat, Governor Harriman told them, "There is a young man who sits among you tonight that would make the best Republican nominee for Governor: Nelson Rockefeller." He said this "jokingly," according to Robert H. Connery and Gerald Benjamin in their 1979 book, *Rockefeller of New York: Executive Power in the Statehouse*. Not long after, Rockefeller did indeed render Harriman a one-term Governor. And yet Harriman may have had the last laugh, though not in the arena of state politics. After Albany, he returned to Washington and worked for John F. Kennedy and Lyndon B. Johnson in high-level posts.

Rockefeller assumed the governorship in 1959, a somewhat liberal Republican in the days before the party's sharp shift to the right. In 1966, he decided to seek legislation against illegal drug use with a reasonably modest plan. By 1973, the party's move to the right was under way, and Rockefeller was contemplating a run for national office. He needed to prove to Nixon-era Republicans that he was sufficiently tough on law-and-order issues, so his drug policy hardened. With drug abuse still on the rise, along with drug addiction and crimes resulting from the drug trade, he proposed severe and unjust laws that demanded mandatory, lengthy prison sentences without parole—up to fifteen years to life for those found guilty of peddling or owning more than a few ounces of a drug, usually cocaine or heroin, even when the perpetrators had no previous prison records or had not been convicted of a violent crime.

The result, in part, was a jobs-creation program for small towns in upstate New York, where prisons were located (and additional population for those towns, albeit as nonvoters, which Republicans could use to create new legislative districts to control the Senate). Widely popular among a large, panicked segment of the general public but generally opposed by liberals, the Senate supported the Rockefeller drug laws 41–14, and the Assembly voted for them 80–65. The bills were signed on May 8, 1973. Despite the laws, the drug scourge continued unabated, and they were no match in the latter half of the 1980s for the crack cocaine epidemic that swept urban areas of the state.

Joseph Persico, who served for eleven years as Rockefeller's chief speechwriter—while Rocky was Governor and later when he was the nation's vice president—said the passage of the drug law revealed Rockefeller's dismissive attitude toward everyone. His "are-you-with-me-or-against-me test of loyalty," Persico called it. How, asked Persico in his biography of Rockefeller, did well-informed staff members "who knew better" remain silent and permit this "congenitally deformed scheme" to become law?

He answered his own question in his book about his former boss. After reading what Irving Janis, a psychologist, had written about "groupthink," Persico concluded, "I never fully understood the psychological milieu in which the chain of errors in Vietnam was forged until I became involved in the Rockefeller drug proposal." It was what happens when there is no one in a policy maker's inner circle willing to dissent or at least raise objections.

At times when Rockefeller failed miserably and cruelly—as during the Attica prison affair of 1971, when many inmates and prison employees were killed during a prison revolt—far too many Democrats in the Legislature looked the other way. They folded again when Rockefeller easily won laws favoring banking, insurance, and finance businesses. Congenitally arrogant, Rockefeller managed to easily outmaneuver his critics in the state. New York voters elected and reelected him from 1959 to 1973, until he departed to serve as Gerald Ford's appointed vice president following Nixon's resignation. His next step was the presidency, a prize that eluded him when right-wing opponents ironically decided that he was still too liberal for a Republican.

All the same, his accomplishments were extensive. Small state colleges were absorbed into the prestigious State University of New York system, with excellent public universities in Albany, Binghamton, Buffalo, and Stony Brook. Smaller colleges, at Brockport, Cortland, Oneonta, Plattsburgh, Purchase, and elsewhere, were transformed into models of liberal arts and specialty schools. Community colleges were opened throughout the state. In Albany, Rockefeller's pet project, the South Mall, later named after him, loomed forty-four stories high with four twenty-three-story towers behind it, including the Department of Motor Vehicles Building, which someone once compared to an ancient temple.

Rockefeller also managed to revolutionize the malfunctioning Long Island Rail Road, the largest commuter railway in the nation, by pouring in money and working deals with the unions, almost overnight changing a troubled line into one of the country's finest. The Metropolitan Transit Authority, the Urban Development Corporation, the Council on the Arts, and an extraordinary number of public authorities (many unaccountable to the Legislature and therefore hugely expensive) were some of his creations. With virtually no significant legislative opposition and widespread public backing, what Rockefeller wanted, Rockefeller got.

Near the end of 1973, Rockefeller departed Albany. His little-known but knowledgeable and long-serving lieutenant governor, Malcolm Wilson, assumed the governorship on December 18, 1973. Wilson had started in the Assembly in 1938, then was tapped to serve as Rockefeller's lieutenant governor in 1959. Rockefeller may well have understood that Wilson knew

far more about the internecine conflicts of Albany than Rockefeller would ever know or care to know, since Rockefeller's own
eyes were on a higher prize. When Rockefeller finally resigned
after serving for fourteen years, Wilson supposedly quipped
that he had been number two "longer than Avis." But he served
as Governor for only slightly more than a year, losing to Hugh
Carey in the November 1974 election—hardly in office long
enough to make a mark. Still, when Wilson died in 2000, his
longtime attorney, William Harrington, summed up his career
by remarking, "When Malcolm spoke, people listened. I don't
think there was anyone more learned about state government
than Malcolm Wilson." Most veterans of Albany agreed.

It is perhaps too early to fully assess the terms of other Governors such as Hugh Carey, Mario Cuomo, and the far blander
George Pataki. Carey, a World War II infantry major and recipient of a Bronze Star, Croix de Guerre, and Combat Infantry
Award, served in Congress from 1961 to 1974, when he resigned to run successfully for Governor of New York. He will
certainly be remembered for his rescue of New York City when
it was threatened with bankruptcy in 1975. He recruited estimable people from the private sector, such as Felix Rohatyn
and Richard Ravitch, to help resolve the problems of over-
spending, overwhelming debt, and fiscal gimmickry.

Cuomo and the Legislature fought battles over ethics in government. Following his landslide victory in 1986, he formed a
state commission (headed by Joseph Califano, formerly a
member of President Carter's cabinet) to look into corruption;
it was scrubbed by the Legislature. Investigate New York City,
not the rest of the state, they demanded. Nor would the Legislature consent to an ethics law for its members. They could
look after their own, they said, and cynically dubbed Cuomo
"St. Mario." When they finally succumbed after a furious

fight, Cuomo rubbed a little salt into their collective wound by adding a provision for regular audits of all state agencies. How effective that has remained over the long run is unclear.

Both Carey and Cuomo were tough enough to resist overwhelming public and political opinion favoring capital punishment. "Bring back the death penalty" was the campaign issue used over and again by politicians running for office; the two of them, however, refused to budge. Some Democrats and very few Republicans stood by them and voted against the death penalty. Republican Senator John Marchi, for example, the longest-serving state senator, consistently voted against the death penalty whether the Governor was a Democrat or a Republican. When Cuomo left office, Pataki reinstated the death penalty, part of his first campaign platform. But in 2005, following a court ruling criticizing the legal language of the legislation enabling capital punishment, the Assembly, spurred mainly by black and Hispanic Democrats from New York City, blocked the restoration of language that was promoted by the State Senate, thereby eliminating the death penalty. Pataki's singular achievement, as he often described it, was no more. Not a single death-row prisoner had been put to death in New York during his term of office.

Pataki had been a state legislator before influential political friends hoisted him into the executive office, where he served three terms. A little-known three-term assemblyman and one-term state senator from Peekskill, he was groomed by Republican powerhouse Senator Alfonse D'Amato to defeat Cuomo, who was running for his fourth term as Governor. He became the first Republican Governor of the state in twenty years and rode an initial wave of popularity among those voters who welcomed his assertive tax-cutting efforts and hard line against crime. He was, for many, a reassuring presence on September

11, 2001, when President George W. Bush and Vice President Dick Cheney were conspicuous by their absence.

Perhaps Pataki's most enduring contribution was that he was always a well-regarded guardian of the state's environment. However, the "three men in a room" syndrome that has so badly damaged democracy in New York State flourished on his watch.

CHAPTER 4

The Big Gerrymander

New York's governorship has changed hands a number of times during the past forty years, alternating between Republicans and Democrats. Moreover, Democrats and Republicans regularly succeed one another as Governor, U.S. senators and representatives, and state attorneys general and comptrollers—proof that New Yorkers are, if not exactly fickle, at least capable of looking beyond mere party labels when they choose the people to whom they entrust the people's business. Such orderly transitions from one party to another are usually seen as a hallmark of a healthy political system that can change course as new trends and challenges arise.

But over the same forty years, there has been little party change at all within New York's State Legislature. Entrenched party majorities dominate the Republican-controlled State Senate and the Democratic-controlled State Assembly. In the Senate, Republicans' current ruling majority consists of 35 seats to the Democrats' 27. In the Assembly, Democrats have increased their margin to 103–47 following the 2002 election, making the Assembly able to override a Governor's veto. The

State Senate has been controlled by the Republicans since 1966. The Assembly has been controlled by the Democrats since 1974.

Like the ebb and flow of ocean tides, the rise and fall in political party fortunes is usually thought to be a natural phenomenon. If so, then there is something unnatural about the parties' hammerlocks on political dominance in their respective chambers. And that something is the way New York carries out its legislative redistricting mandate every ten years.

New York, like every other state (except Colorado and Texas, where Republican state legislative leaders have forced mid-decade redistricting for blatantly partisan purposes), redraws its legislative district lines once a decade, following the outcome of the national census. The purpose is to comply with the requirements of U.S. Supreme Court decisions upholding the principle of "one person, one vote." Americans have always been a people on the move, and if electoral district lines were to remain fixed and unchanging while people move in and out of electoral districts, we would soon find that some elected officials would represent more people in their district, and other officials fewer people. The result would be that voters in more populous districts (of, for example, one million voters) would find their votes diluted, compared to voters who live in a less populated district (comprising, say, a half million voters).

To make sure that every voter has equal representation in Albany, within two years of every national census each house in the New York State Legislature appoints a task force to determine which Senate and Assembly districts have gained and which have lost population. After analyzing the numbers, the task force is then supposed to recommend how district lines should be modified so that the new boundaries produce roughly equal numbers of voters in each district.

That's the theory, and given the power of today's computers, it should be easy to pour data about the state's voting population into a program and have it spit out any number of plans for districts containing roughly equal numbers of voters. In practice, however, redistricting is far more complicated. The main complication in New York is that the party in power in each chamber of the Legislature makes sure that new district lines are drawn so that as many of its members as possible keep their seats—and, if possible, a few members of the opposing party are defeated and replaced with one of their own members.

Giving the ruling party in each chamber of the Legislature the power to set district lines is akin to contracting out construction of a fox-proof henhouse to the chicken-stealing fox. It recalls the origin of the word *gerrymander.* In 1811, the Democratic Governor of Massachusetts, Eldridge Gerry, signed into law a bill that redrew a congressional district in his state with the intention of carving out a Democratic majority in an area long loyal to the Federalist Party. The lines of the new district were said to resemble a salamander, and a newspaper editorial cartoonist renamed the most unusual object a "gerrymander," in honor of the Governor who invented it.

In our time, a number of other states, Iowa prominent among them, hand the task of redrawing district lines to independent, nonpartisan commissions. These commissions feed into computers such factors as census data about population shifts, Voting Rights Act requirements to ensure minority representation, and other demographic information, then recommend objective district lines. It's a nonpartisan way to avoid conflicts of interest and self-interest in a critically important political process.

The 2000 federal census showed that some parts of New York State had gained population and other parts had lost population, making it necessary to reconfigure district lines for the Senate and the Assembly. Due to a complicated formula adopted in 1894 that remains enshrined in the state's constitution, it was determined that creation of additional seats—perennially Republican—was warranted for upstate New York. The reason is that the Republican-controlled Senate wants to maintain its majority.

As it stood up to that point, small towns in upstate New York were already the home of a large, imported prison population that cannot vote but which is nonetheless counted for the purpose of the federal census and for state redistricting. The state's 1990s prison boom thus benefits Republican upstate districts while weakening the legislative power and presence of heavily Democratic and densely populated New York City, where the majority of inmates formerly lived. About one-third of 1990's entire population growth upstate was due to the boom in prison cells. This use of the prison population for politically charged redistricting purposes prompted Roland Nicholson Jr., chairman of the Fortune Society, to comment on "the resemblance between this system and early America under slavery, when a slave counted as three-fifths of a person for census purposes but had no rights whatsoever."

The recent census-triggered decision to create another additional Senate seat for upstate New York meant that boundaries throughout the state had to be reconfigured to ensure that the population in each district would remain roughly equal. If New York had in place a redistricting system such as Iowa's nonpartisan Legislative Service Bureau, then voters in the Senate district to which I was initially elected in 1996 might have been spared the disaster that Senate Republicans visited upon them soon after the decision to give the Senate an additional seat.

When redistricting is called for, Iowa's Legislative Service Bureau, which was created in 1980, is required to formulate three sets of plans for submission to the state Legislature. During the planning phase, the bureau can call upon advice from a five-member commission, four of whose participants are chosen by party caucuses in the Legislature. (The other commissioners select a fifth member, the commission's chairperson.) The Iowa bureau is insulated from political pressures that commissioners might wish to exert by the fact that the commission can provide advice only when the bureau requests it.

When drawing up districts, the Iowa bureau follows four principles, ranked in order of importance: equality of population in each district; contiguity; avoiding, insofar as possible, splitting city and county boundary lines while keeping its State House districts within State Senate districts and State Senate districts within congressional districts; and, finally, attempting to make new districts as compact as possible. Most significantly, the Iowa statute that created the bureau ensures that its decisions will not be swayed by partisan party interest by forbidding the bureau to use data about party affiliation and results from previous elections in making its redistricting proposals.

After the bureau has drafted its redistricting plans, its first proposal is submitted for public comment to three open meetings held around the state. The Iowa Legislature then votes on whether to accept or reject it. If that plan is rejected, the bureau then submits its second plan and, if need be, its third. Should these be rejected, the Legislature must draw up its own plan by September 1 of the year following the national decennial census; otherwise, Iowa's State Supreme Court takes over the task of formulating new districts, based on the principles of equal population, compactness, and contiguity. A measure of the Iowa system's success is that in the twenty-five years the

Legislative Service Bureau has existed, its first proposal has been rejected only once—in 2001—and in that instance the Legislature adopted the bureau's second plan. The state's Supreme Court has yet to intervene to take control or responsibility for mandating a redistricting plan.

In the absence of a nonpartisan redistricting commission such as Iowa's, the task of proposing new State Senate and Assembly districts in New York is in the hands of the State Legislative Task Force on Demographic Research and Reapportionment (or, as it is commonly referred to in Albany-speak, LATFOR). Created in 1978, following a number of court challenges that found previous redistricting plans had violated the one person, one vote guarantee of the U.S. Constitution, LATFOR is structured to give the impression that it is nonpartisan. It is, however, bipartisan, and given the fact that each chamber of the Legislature is solidly controlled by a different political party, "bipartisan" means, in effect, that each party lets the other one do as it wishes in the chamber it dominates. And the bottom-line wish of each party in redistricting matters is to maintain and, if at all possible, increase its already healthy majority in the chamber it controls.

LATFOR plugged the 2000 federal census numbers into its computers and made a pretense of seeking the public's advice before it divulged its proposal about how the new sixty-two-member State Senate's districts should be configured. Between May 2001 and March 2002, LATFOR held hearings in major cities upstate (Buffalo, Rochester, Syracuse, Albany, and Binghamton), in each of New York City's five boroughs, and in suburban Westchester and Suffolk counties. There was never any question, however, that the fix was in from the start, and any doubt I may have had that partisan political advantage was the driving force behind the new lines vanished when the Senate's final redistricting plan was unveiled in April 2002.

The heart of the Senate district to which I was first elected in 1996 was centered in Borough Park, Bensonhurst, Brighton, Windsor Terrace, and Coney Island in Brooklyn. However, when the new Senate plan was unveiled, it was patently clear that those basic, objective principles of redistricting, such as creating and maintaining compact and contiguous districts, had been thrown out the window. LATFOR split Borough Park and parceled it out among five disparate districts. Now, instead of having to deal with only one or two state senators in order to have their neighborhood's interests represented in Albany, Borough Park residents found themselves "diluted" among five state senators. Having fewer Borough Park residents in each of the new districts of roughly equal size meant, in effect, that Borough Park's voice in each district became fainter and easier to discount when its residents needed to call Albany's attention to a problem.

Not only was the Borough Park neighborhood greatly reduced as part of my district in the new plan, but the boundaries outlining my Senate seat were also redrawn by a master jigsaw puzzle creator. Iowa requires that its state legislative districts be compact and avoid crossing county lines irrationally. But my new district, instead of being entirely within the borough of Brooklyn, was now attached to Staten Island by a thin, four-mile-long corridor running along a highway.

Clearly, however, Republican members of LATFOR were primarily interested in keeping or extending their party's control of the Senate, and proceeded on the basis that if compactness mattered to anyone in the new district, they'd simply have to file a lawsuit challenging the new lines, with the under-

standing that by the time the suit was heard and appealed in
state and federal courts, the results of the 2002 election would
be a fait accompli.

No voters in Brooklyn or Staten Island sued to challenge the
underlying partisan motives of LATFOR's redistricting plan.
But some civic-minded souls in Long Island's Nassau County
did, and a pretrial discovery motion exposed the blatantly political goals behind the new Senate lines. At issue in the Nassau
suit was the claim on the part of civil rights advocates that,
under provisions of the federal Voting Rights Act, there was a
sufficiently compact minority population on Long Island to
mandate that New York State create a district in which minority voters would have an opportunity to decide the outcome of
a Senate election. Given that population changes throughout
the state required that one or more new Senate seats had to be
added, thus requiring all Senate district boundaries to be redrawn, this request would have been fairly easy to accommodate.

Such was the farthest thing from the intentions of the Republican members and staff of LATFOR. A key player in
LATFOR's decisions was Mark Burgeson, an assistant to State
Senator Dean Skelos, who in turn owed his appointment as
LATFOR's co-chairman to Bruno. In a memo sent to Skelos in
June 2001, almost a year before the new district lines were announced, Burgeson discussed the possibility that a total of
sixty-three Senate seats could be created, not the sixty-two that
were eventually announced. And, Burgeson noted, one option
for a sixty-third Senate district was to locate it on Long Island,
to accommodate minority voters in Nassau and Suffolk counties. But having raised the prospect, Burgeson then shot it
down. "The *only* reason to go to 63," he told Skelos, "is to

strengthen the Long Island delegation by combining politically undesirable areas in the extra district."

When a three-judge panel of the U.S. District Court for the Southern District of New York finally issued its decision about the suit in March 2004—a year and a half after the state's 2002 elections were held—the court noted that blatantly partisan calculations had driven Burgeson's recommendation. "Plainly," the court wrote, "the political majority [i.e., the Republican Party, which controls the Senate] would have been strengthened in existing districts by removing voters not of that party [i.e., Democrats] from current districts and placing them in a new district. However, Burgeson concluded that adding another district would have resulted in the loss of a Republican incumbent depending on how it was done, and it probably would not have provided an extra Republican seat."

Nonetheless, the court, led by Chief Circuit Judge John Mercer Walker Jr., a Republican appointed to the bench by his uncle, former President George Herbert Walker Bush, ruled against the suit, letting stand a redistricting plan that it recognized as being distorted to serve partisan political ends. Even a coalition of clergy and community leaders who met with Senator Skelos to protest the redistricting were told that he was instructed to make no changes and make certain that a new Republican senator be elected from Brooklyn and that Democratic senator Carl Kruger be given a permanently safe seat.

After my nine years in the New York State Senate, and having stood for and won election five times—the last despite an attempt by the Senate's Republican junta to redistrict me into defeat—it is clear to me that obsessions over party self-preservation trump any and every consideration whenever decisions are made in either the Senate or the Assembly. So long as a mandatory process such as redistricting, which is a matter of protecting the right of voters to make sure that their votes count equally, is left to a body of political appointees such as LATFOR, New Yorkers will enjoy only a pretense of democratic rights and liberties.

LATFOR is only a fig leaf, an attempt to hide what is essentially a corrupt bargain between party bosses to let their respective legislative troops remain occupying powers in each chamber of the Legislature.

Deadlock in Albany will be broken only when redistricting is taken out of the hands of those who have a self-interest in the outcome—meaning partisan elected politicians and their staffs—and given over to an independent, nonpartisan commission that operates with the public's interests uppermost in its mind.

CHAPTER 5

Lobbyists (and Legislators) Gone Wild

Many state legislators I came to know were decent and conscientious. They suffered unfairly from the low esteem in which politicians are generally held by the public, due to the actions of a minority of them. A handful of state legislators and their top staff people, of course, are neither ethical nor conscientious, tainting the rest of us. It is unfair to judge the rest of us by them, but it is a fact of life.

It was not human foible but rather the way the system worked that offended my particular sensibilities and perspective. On and on, year after year, Albany's processes and practices continue in ways that obscure how money is spent, how patronage jobs are handed out, how debate and public input are minimized, and how a tiny number of influential people make the decisions in Albany. The system is broken, and occasional reforms, while welcome, are grudging, rare, and limited in scope.

The strange ways of Albany first struck me in my freshman year, when I began a conversation with two security guards. The two gray-haired gentlemen were retired state troopers who had been stationed in the State Capitol building after

9/11. Both men stood ramrod straight in a stone hallway under a towering, vastly impressive ceiling. At the end of our chat, just to be friendly and respectful, I asked them for their names.

"I'm Jack, and he's John, Senator," one said.

"Since you have asked me to call you by your first names, please call me Seymour, not Senator."

"Yes, Senator," they replied, almost in unison.

The following day, one of my colleagues, who overheard part of the hallway conversation, told me that if the pair had called me Seymour, as I preferred, rather than Senator, and if that had come to be known to their superiors, it could have jeopardized their jobs.

Not even a legislative staff member, I subsequently learned, was permitted under Senate tradition to call a senator by his or her first name or even last name. When my staff assistants and I wanted to have a confidential talk in Albany we had to close the door to be able to call one another by our first names. But if we met on the Senate floor, amid the rows of plush leather chairs, they sometimes referred to me, formally and stiffly, as Senator Lachman.

One initial member of my staff, whom I considered a friend, turned to me on the floor of the Senate without much thought and said, "Hey, Seymour, whaddaya think of this?" Hearing the outburst, one of my colleagues in the Senate, a Democrat who was known for berating the staff and requiring them to run personal errands, demanded to know the staff member's name—and to receive an apology.

New York's senators are made to feel they are very powerful. Some buy into it. I did, too, at first. But the forced pretense is actually just one of the ways that the house leaders stay in control of the legislators. Legislators enjoy the perquisites, and the

all-important aura, of power. All sorts of inane rules of conduct protect their place in the hierarchy.

The reality, though, is that most individual state senators
and Assembly members have little power. Instead, they must
bend to the whims of their chamber's leaders in order to pre-
serve their member items, office supplies, staffs, car service,
and committee assignments. They're expected to hold their
end up in this charade and, as part of it, to be addressed only by
their title, whether privately or in the presence of others.

There has, in fact, long been a high degree of institutional
tolerance in Albany for this sort of artifice, not to mention for
corruption. That is more damaging to the character of legislators, even well-intentioned ones, and to the state as a whole,
than many voters realize. Periods of public apathy also don't
help.

The overall problem in the Capitol, though, begins and ends
with money, to a greater degree than one might suspect even in
an especially corrupt and cynical era in the history of state and
national government. To frame the problem, one must start
and probably end with fund-raising, the bread, butter, and singular preoccupation of politicians who wish to remain on the
Albany dole for any period longer than just one term.

On a Monday night in February 2005, the Republicans
who run the Senate and the Democrats who preside over the
Assembly convened separate fund-raisers in the very same
Albany hotel. In fact, the fund-raisers were in adjoining
ballrooms.

This was just perfect for the lobbyists and their clients who
feed off Albany, since many could cross the invisible partisan
divide without having to get in their cars. Indeed, to show their
support for the legislators of both political parties, they just

walked their checkbooks from the New York State Senate Republican Committee fete, hosted by Senator Joe Bruno, over to the adjoining soiree, hosted by Assemblyman Sheldon Silver. Statehouse-based reporter Michael Cooper, who covered the accidentally—yet conveniently—conjoined events in an article for the *New York Times*, wrote, "The fact that it was Valentine's Day did not keep many big names away from the two parties."

Alexander Grannis, a Manhattan Democratic assemblyman, sounded just as sardonic; he had long been critical of Albany's tradition of holding hundreds of fund-raisers a year and typically convening them while the Legislature was in session—a slippery slope that twenty-seven states, but not New York, have banned or limited. Grannis whimsically suggested there be more joint fund-raisers, and that they be held in the basement complex of the Capitol, the site of annual trade fairs where hawkers sing their wares.

"Each member would have a booth," he told Cooper. "It would be easier for the lobbyist, easier for the member, better for the waistline."

The Legislature started its 2005 session by passing a relative handful of minor reforms—including one requiring, for the first time, that lobbying of state agencies be made public instead of being kept secret, as had been the case for as long as I was in Albany and for as long as anyone could remember.

Obviously, this minor reform was long overdue. New York State has more registered lobbyists per legislator—a ratio of eighteen to one—than any other state in the country, according to a 2005 report by the Center for Public Integrity in Washington. In addition, gifts and honorariums that lobbyists gave to lawmakers were barely restricted until early 2006—the lobbyists had to make sure that any single gift was under $75, but that could mean a $74.99 breakfast, $74.99 lunch, and $74.99 dinner, all in the same day. But the state requirement that lobbyists register is merely a tentative first step, because it doesn't interrupt the influence of the special interests, which use lobbyists, campaign cash, and personal access to the Big Three who make the big-money decisions. When necessary, many can, and do, retain Sheldon Silver's former top aide Patricia Lynch, now a successful lobbyist, or former Speaker Mel Miller, or former state Republican Party chairman Bill Powers, or Bruno's son, Kenneth—he has since quit working as a lobbyist—who are all set up in the same lucrative field, enriching statehouse-linked business clients and themselves.

In the decade I spent in the State Capitol, the number of lobbyists more than doubled, to approximately four thousand individuals. The amount of money that New York State lobbyists earn has more than quadrupled, to more than $150 million annually, one of the highest statehouse windfalls in the nation. As mentioned, the top lobbyists are powerhouses, given their long-standing ties to the powers that be in Albany. This is why, for example, pharmaceutical companies pour millions into lobbying and contributions to legislators, the better to ensure their effectiveness when the moment comes to promote, stall, or defeat measures of interest to them, time and again resisting efforts to limit the drugs covered by Medicaid for budgetary reasons, as other states have done. The industry's ability to sway the Legislature through lobbying and campaign largesse may help explain why Medicaid costs in New York, population 19 million, far exceed those of every other state, including California's, population 35 million. Fraud and waste are also excessive in New York, abetted by the lack of political will to oversee Medicaid spending. Indeed, both Spitzer and Suozzi have been critical of the Legislature's 2006 budget for not dealing at all with Medicaid reform.

Recently, some lobbying firms have attempted to influence the Democratic Assembly and the Republican Senate by becoming bipartisan and hiring former leaders of both parties. For me, a July 23, 2005, account by New York *Daily News* reporter Greg B. Smith rang numbingly familiar. It began: "A development team that includes a former aide to Governor Pataki and a major donor to his campaigns has been fast-tracked to build luxury condos in Brooklyn, the *Daily News* has found." The team included Thomas Murphy, former head of the state Dormitory Authority, and the insurance company AIG, which had donated $100,000 to Pataki in the past three years, according to the story.

Along with a developer, Robert Levine, the group planned to build 450 condos at 360 Furman Street on the Brooklyn waterfront, inside a park slated to replace piers and warehouses owned by the state.

Smith continued as follows: "The state says the condos will help pay for the new park, but neighbors are baffled by the lightning-quick pace of development of a taxpayer-backed park they say will serve as landscaping for affluent condo owners."

Said one Brooklyn Heights resident as quoted in the piece, "This is everything we fought against, this whole idea of getting housing." And a member of the Cobble Hill Neighborhood Association said that the net effect of the state's plan was to replace recreational areas that would serve the general public with landscaping "meant to sell apartments."

It was the Pataki-controlled Empire State Development Corporation, the agency building it, that first proposed legislation in April 2005 that made the condo plan part of the agency's planned Brooklyn Bridge Park, according to Smith's account.

"The agency said it believed the bill was necessary because the area is zoned for commercial use only," he wrote, adding that the development team hired Murphy to lobby for the legislation. Murphy worked for the lobbying firm run by William Powers, the former head of the state Republican Party who was instrumental in Pataki's first gubernatorial victory in 1994.

The Assembly in April 2005 passed the bill, making 360 Furman Street part of a state park. The State Senate added its approval that June.

Adding to the sense of a community cut out of the loop, Smith noted that the development property is owned by New York–based AIG in partnership with developer Levine; AIG donated $40,000 to Friends of Pataki on March 29, 2004, days before the state revealed it was in talks with Levine about the Brooklyn condo plan.

So this story went. It was all legal, of course.

But in Albany, that's the way it goes.

Former U.S. senator Al D'Amato, who plucked Pataki from relative obscurity and rode him to statewide victory over the liberal Mario Cuomo in 1994, was paid $500,000 by a business client in 1999 for making a single lobbying phone call to the Metropolitan Transit Authority, which helped his client secure a loan for $230 million from the agency to continue building its new headquarters in Manhattan. At the time, the building project had fallen behind schedule and was plagued by millions in cost overruns.

Though nothing illegal was found by the agency's inspector

general, the scenario was about as cozy as it gets, even in a state where upward of $120 million a year is spent on lobbying to secure state contracts. D'Amato is Pataki's political mentor, Pataki has a great measure of control of the MTA, and its executive director, Katherine Lapp, is Pataki's former coordinator of criminal justice services.

Amid the wheeling and dealing, voters without the capital—political or financial—to hire an enormously influential former U.S. senator for access to senior decision makers are out of luck, and are in fact left largely in the dark, as were legislators such as myself, who usually had to read the newspapers to try to find out what was going on and were handed complex bills to vote on with just hours to go before the predetermined voting went ahead. We were lucky when we had two days to read hundreds of pages of legislation. We were human rubber stamps in an environment where people may only refer to us as "Senator this" or "Senator that."

Senator Liz Krueger, who represents the eastern half of Manhattan, tells the story of approaching the Republican leadership in the Senate in 2003 with enough formal commitments, or buck slips, from Republicans for a bill that would require health insurers to cover mental health services for children. The bill, Timothy's Law, was named for a depressive twelve-year-old boy who killed himself after his cash-strapped parents ended his drug treatment and counseling. It was modeled after similar coverage available in thirty other states. The leadership refused to carry it, heeding the interests of the insurance companies. Indeed, one man, Bruno, prevented it from ever reaching committee for debate, much less a floor vote. The Democrats in Albany, Krueger noted, had been supportive of such legislation for years.

As Krueger tells it, "I went into the doghouse for twelve

months, and I can tell you, it's not a good place to be." No bills from her were allowed, nor were member items allocated to her district. She became an outcast for daring to go up against Senator Bruno. "Alice in Wonderland" was how she characterized the experience. And it understandably left her feeling resolved to work the electoral system, with other Democrats, to eliminate the Republicans' majority hold on the Senate in the coming years and try to create a fully Democratic-led Legislature.

I don't know whether they'll succeed or whether it will help change the way the system operates. I personally feel reformist energies at this moment need to go into changing the way the Legislature works, not who fills the majority of seats.

When the long battle for the 2002 leadership began, I initially supported the efforts of the incumbent Senate Minority Leader to remain in power. Indeed, I gave Martin Connor my word only after the progressive Senator Paterson himself telephoned me on a Friday and told me—for motives I don't know and can't discern—that he was not seeking the powerful Democratic berth and was interested instead in supporting Connor. I, said Paterson, should do the same.

That morning, though, a *New York Post* item had appeared questioning his supposed challenge to Connor. "Don't believe it, it's not true," Paterson, then the Deputy Minority Leader of the Senate, called me at home and told me. "I am supporting Senator Connor for the leadership."

I said to Paterson, to whom I felt close personally and professionally, "David, are you saying I should support Connor?" He said, "Absolutely."

Over the weekend, I received phone calls from many people, such as Manhattan Democratic senator Eric Schneiderman, asking me to support what they said was *Paterson's* push to seize control of the Democratic leadership post in the Senate—all in the name of reforming the Legislature. A donnybrook was getting under way, despite Paterson's assurances to me to the contrary. Schneiderman called, as did other important politicians, to seek my vote for Paterson, saying the vote was going to be close and if I could help put Paterson over the top, it would be helpful to my future in Albany. He intimated that I would be in line for a more influential position under new leadership.

I had already pledged my support to Connor at the recommendation of Paterson and felt, as a matter of my own sense of integrity and not out of any limited political alliance I might have had with Connor at various junctures, that I could not easily go back on my word at that advanced stage. Besides, I believed I had been misled by the very man who Albany's reform-minded younger Turks, including Schneiderman and Krueger, were lining up behind.

I mentioned to Schneiderman that I had spoken with Paterson on Friday, and what he had told me. Why hadn't Paterson called me back since then to say he was in fact seeking the post? Well, Schneiderman responded, things had gotten a bit hairy since then.

Not good enough, I said. Nor was I interested any longer in a promotion or perks.

Paterson finally called me Tuesday. He said my vote was important to him now. Connor's fair-weather allies in our party had fled to Paterson as soon as they sensed Connor's ship was foundering. I did, too, with some reluctance because of the process used. This was a day before Paterson's victory was, as expected, sealed by a decision by Queens County Democrats to get behind him in force. Before I did so—if only to salvage what was left of my pride—I called Connor to let him know of my change of mind. I felt that a vote for Connor at that point would have done nothing but consign me to irrelevancy for the rest of my tenure. However, I also believed that Paterson would be more inclusive and collegial than Connor, and I had always been closer to Paterson than to Connor.

Depressed because he had been outmaneuvered, Connor told me that I was the only senator who had given him the courtesy of a warning and explanation. The rest had simply deserted.

I was not exactly, in any case, left in good standing with the triumphant pro-Paterson legislators. Most of them, I suspect, got behind him in part because they believed that the Democrats could do things better than the Republicans if only they could take control of the Senate and therefore hold both houses in Albany. While that partisan goal is understandable from their point of view, and perhaps realizable before the next redistricting in 2012, since the Republicans currently have but a 35–27 lead in the Senate over the Democrats, my own view is that wholesale structural change is what is needed in Albany and is the only thing that will make a meaningful difference, regardless of which party has the upper hand. No leader in either party will voluntarily give up control—and it is the mandatory ceding and dispersal of their power that is needed.

So the reformers want reform. I have no doubt of that. It is only their strategy to win control for the Democrats that I quarrel with. Liz Krueger, for example, deserves great credit for subsequently suing the Governor and the leaders of both houses in late 2004 together with Newburgh assemblyman Thomas Kirwan, a Republican, and the Urban Justice Center in Manhattan. They charged that the rules and practices of the two legislative bodies make a mockery of state and federal constitutional principles by denying minority-party representatives (Democrats in the Senate, like Krueger, and Republicans in the Assembly, like Kirwan) a "fair opportunity" to represent their constituents and make the voices of their constituents heard.

"In New York," the complaint correctly said, "the speaker and majority leader effectively control the funds available for each member's staff. In addition, they control the members' use of office space. The speaker and majority leader also effectively control each member's necessary expenses, such as computers, mailing and printing costs for newsletters and travel reimbursements. The majority party leadership also imposes content restrictions on minority members' publications as a condition to funding the printing and postage of such publications, in an effort to deter vigorous debate of legislation."

The suit, still pending in the state courts as of this writing, goes on as follows: "The speaker and Majority Leader make more funds and resources available to members who are members of the majority party, than to members of the minority party who have equal responsibility. The differences in stipends and other resources are gross and are not reasonably related to differences in need, but rather related solely to differences in party enrollment. They are adopted with the purpose, intent, and effect of punishing constituents who elected a representative in the Assembly who is a Republican or a representative in the Senate who is a Democrat."

In 1990, a series of scandals centered on New York's City Hall led to the formation of a state blue-ribbon panel that demanded a series of reforms.

"In our view," the New York State Commission on Government Integrity said in response to the "city for sale" scandals involving bribes and kickbacks to elected officials, and state and city dollars, "the leaders of both major parties have failed the citizens of New York by not insisting upon much-needed ethics reforms. . . . Instead, partisan, personal and vested interests have been allowed to come before larger public interests."

I found out in my time in Albany that little has changed, despite the series of reports that resulted from those particularly corrupt years. In the feverish, cash-fueled, and chronic competition for contracts and legislation to benefit individuals, unions, organizations, industries, and other interest groups, Albany still puts up few obstacles to conflicts of interest or favoritism.

The system continues to let the campaign money flow in with few impediments or rules, and rewards the most generous givers, such as the 450 political action committees that contributed more than $13.5 million in 2004 alone; nearly half of that total came from just sixteen PACs, topped by the New York State United Teachers and followed by the largest health care workers union, lawyers, doctors, and insurance companies.

While corporate donations have been banned for candidates in federal races, as well as those in New York City, the sky's the limit in New York State's elections, practically speaking. True, there is a state law that theoretically restricts corporations to $5,000 a year in political donations. But companies ignore the cap by having subsidiaries give, while many legislators, including some of my Democratic and Republican colleagues, ignore the rules for ethical conduct by accepting free rides and other gifts from influence peddlers.

Corporations also lavish the party campaign organizations' housekeeping accounts with donations, which can be embarrassing, as when some of the donors' money is paying the $50,000 annual salary of a personal assistant, food shopper, and housekeeper for the Governor's wife, as the *New York Post*'s Albany reporter Fred Dicker wrote in early 2005.

New York State has a rickety, backward system for keeping track of campaign contributions. As already indicated, state law limits companies to $5,000 a year. That's the total amount of contributions in one calendar year a company may make for state and local elections. The problem is, there is no central computerized data bank in Albany for all contributions around the state. Records are kept county by county. Thus, politicians and contributors enjoy the safety of relative privacy—it is more than a little difficult for anyone to try to "follow the money." When Common Cause and the New York Public Interest Research Group did so in 2003, they found that ninety-six companies had topped the $5,000 cap by distributing their money throughout the state.

By the good-government groups' own reckoning, the total was just a piece of the overall problem, since records in many counties were ill maintained or difficult to read. But one engineering company wrote checks adding up to $17,646 to sixty-five election committees. Another firm, in Nassau County, spread $18,575 among twenty-one election committees.

What did the State Board of Elections do after it received the report? It began to investigate, then dropped the case, citing a lack of staff. And the Legislature and Governor conveniently did nothing to change that.

Because the link between big-money contributors and the public benefits they derive is not always crystal clear, it is an issue that rarely arouses sustained public outrage. Pay-to-play arrangements are typically based on tacit understandings. If you want a state agency or a politician to return your phone call or consider your request for a state contract, regulatory change, or legislation, you make a contribution of some significance, show up at the campaign fund-raiser, or hire the right lobbyist or consultant. (Lobbyists' gifts to state lawmakers were restricted to a maximum of $75 per year starting in early 2006, but not contributors' donations. I can recall when a prominent physician who had contributed $250 to my campaign wanted to donate the same amount to the Assembly Speaker's campaign fund; he was told by a mutual friend of ours to add an extra zero and make it $2,500 if he wanted to have any input with the Speaker.)

"The loopholes and soft money contributions are the dark side of New York's political system," a *Daily News* editorial pointed out, in a complaint often stated. "The public may clamor for reform, but if the big money boys balk, reform dies abornin'. Look at Medicaid. It needs major fixes." (In fact, it represented the largest single expenditure in the $105 billion state budget of 2005 and the $112 billion budget of 2006.) "Nothing has been done, however, because reform opponents—hospitals and the health workers unions—have bought a boatload of support in Albany."

If anyone thinks that the fault lies with either party alone, and not equally with both of them, consider that the Senate has long viewed the cash-flush doctors' lobby as their client, and the Assembly has looked upon personal-injury lawyers as theirs; Silver is himself a personal-injury lawyer. Governor Pataki scrambled those long-standing arrangements by handing the state's largest, and traditionally Democratic, health care workers union a raise during his 2002 reelection campaign, robbing his Democratic opponent, then-Comptroller H. Carl McCall, of the union's political support. The cost of the raise to taxpayers was well over $1 billion, and it came during a decline in the state's economic condition.

Neither party, moreover, believes in fair and competitive legislative elections. This is also evidenced by the nearly unbridled influence of campaign money, year after year. Why did

Pataki insist on listing campaign contributors in his campaign finance filings alphabetically by first names instead of by surnames? That made it challenging, to say the least, for good-government groups, journalists, and members of the public to keep track of the Governor's financial backing. Fortunately, the outcry was loud enough for Pataki to switch to listing by surname.

But then, New York's Governor, Assembly Speaker, and Senate Majority Leader have shown time and again, and especially as it concerns campaign money and competitive elections and the minority party within their respective houses, that they aren't interested in anything that would result in a significant diminution of their influence over what gets done in Albany.

So we are left with a series of untoward outcomes, among them sky-high campaign contribution limits; easy transfers from one political committee to another; mushrooming campaign fund-raising during the legislative session; late, limited, or scrambled disclosure of contributors; poor enforcement by the chronically underfunded and ill-equipped Board of Elections; frequent use of campaign donations for junkets, country club memberships, flowers, leased cars, swimming pool covers, and even cat food and trips to the vet (as *Newsday* reported in 2000); growing influence of lobbyists (who spent $140 million lobbying the legislature in 2004—a record); and heavy reliance on special interest groups for election funds. It shocked even some seasoned politicians when it was discovered in the summer of 2005 and the winter of 2006 that several *former* elected officials were still using their campaign funds for personal items such as car payments, meals, and cell phone calls.

I suppose I shouldn't have been shocked myself by the coda to Guy Velella's long political career in politics, or the Senate Majority Leader's response to that coda. But I, like many others, was dismayed by the seeming arrogance of both men.

Velella had been a high-ranking, well-liked Bronx/Westchester Republican state senator and county leader. Throughout his three decades in elected office he wielded his clout to garner contracts for political cronies while bringing home the pork for his district. He held a safe Senate seat for eighteen years. He was a fixture, a classic insider.

So it remained until Velella and two associates were charged in 2002 with a twenty-five-count indictment alleging the senator had taken at least $137,000—and allegedly solicited $250,000—in return for steering public works contracts to those who paid bribes.

The indictment covered 1995 to 2000. In 2004, Velella pleaded guilty to one count of bribery and agreed to serve a year in jail. But he was abruptly released after less than twelve weeks, when a virtually unheard-of New York City panel called the Local Conditional Release Commission granted him freedom. Even Mayor Michael Bloomberg initially commented that he had never heard of the commission or that his office had appointed members to it. It had never been the focus of press coverage. Still, someone had apparently known about it and pulled some strings with its members for Velella. But after weeks of embarrassing headlines and outcry, Velella's jail break was rescinded, and he was forced to go back to jail.

With the blessings of Joe Bruno, much of the $292,500 Velella had paid his lawyer by the spring of 2004, and as much as $100,000 additional thereafter, was given to him in individual donations of $7,500 from many fellow legislators who dipped into their own campaign war chests a year before he pleaded guilty. The Senate leadership also added $10,450 to Velella's annual pension while he was serving his prison term.

Bruno was also among nearly three dozen people who wrote to the Local Conditional Release Commission requesting Velella's release, stating that he had suffered enough ("He is no longer a senator, he is no longer able to practice law, he has been financially hurt, and really publicly disgraced").

From time to time, we Democratic senators were asked by our leaders to contribute to the Senate Democratic Campaign Committee. When in 2000 I decided to give $10,000 instead of the expected $30,000, a leading member of then Senate Minority Leader Martin Connor's staff told me, in no uncertain terms, that my contribution had been a disappointment and would be noted by higher-ups when it came to such matters as committee assignments, member items, and other leadership-controlled assistance.

Needless to say, when Republican legislators in the Senate and Assembly were asked to ante up even for an indicted member of their party such as Velella, most but not all did what they were told, without exception or complaint. The press—which has played a crucial and admirable role in examining the hidden recesses of Albany's doings—reported the state Board of Elections opinion, saying it is perfectly fine to pay legal defense bills with campaign funds when charges are related to the "holding of public office." The *Rochester Democrat and Chronicle* asked rhetorically in an editorial, "Is that a loophole?" Then it replied to its own question: "No. It's a hula hoop."

As Bruno passed the hat for his indicted colleague, Liz Krueger and other legislators decided it was time to bring attention to the absurd fact that elected officials in Albany who commit felonies are still entitled to receive their pension—in Velella's case, it came to $80,000 a year.

"This is about making a simple statement to present and future New York elected officials," Krueger said in announcing a bill inspired by the sordid affair. "It is simply unconscionable for elected officials who violate their oaths of office by committing felonies to receive pensions that are funded by taxpaying New Yorkers. You broke the law. You forfeited that right."

Naturally, the bill, which was a sound and fair-minded idea that the public would have sensibly applauded, didn't get far. Such is the fate of most reform measures in the Empire State, unless the leadership in both houses feels its back is to the wall.

Blair Horner, one of the Capitol's most effective and experienced government watchdogs, happened to be in Minnesota attending a 1998 conference on Big Tobacco, after the tobacco industry had deposited records of its lobbying and gift giving nationwide as a result of the industry's lengthy legal battles with the states. Horner, more than six feet tall, boyish-faced, and bespectacled, came of age in the politically progressive 1960s, the decade of take-it-to-the-streets (and to-the-courts) activism. He is the legislative director of the New York Public Interest Research Group, the good-government lobby in Albany, and has held the position since 1987.

Horner was just curious enough to take a look at the tobacco files. He took a taxi to the warehouse where the industry documents were archived. What he discovered in that Minnesota warehouse touched off one of Albany's more illuminating scandals of recent years.

One "astonishing" document, as Horner would later write in a lengthy account for NYPIRG with his intrepid colleague Michelle Stern, was a Tobacco Institute budget indicating that in 1995 the trade group had spent $287,700 on the "New York Preemption Plan"—an expenditure that was not reflected in legally required reports of legislative lobbying expenses filed with New York State.

In the 1980s and early 1990s, the administration of Governor Mario Cuomo had been unfriendly to the tobacco industry. The conservative Pataki's election in 1994 represented an opening for the industry to stave off and reverse the anti-smoking momentum in New York and around the country. Not surprisingly, the company quickly deposited $25,000 in Pataki's inaugural account, which at the time was secret, and launched a lobbying effort to roll back the state's anti-smoking ordinances.

Then, in May 1995, Bruno had a meeting with Philip Morris chief executive officer Geoffrey Bible, senior vice president Ellen Merlo, and the company's top Albany lobbyist, Sharon Portnoy, at Philip Morris's New York City offices. In a follow-up letter to Senator Bruno, Merlo wrote, "Sharon has been singing your praises for quite some time, it's wonderful to know that the leadership in this state is taking a pro-business approach. As said in our meeting, working together we can accomplish a great deal. We all took comfort in the message that you had to deliver."

Of course, as Horner and Stern recounted, the public would never know how Bruno reacted or what his supposedly comforting message was. But on June 12, 1995, the all-powerful Senate Committee on Rules, totally controlled by him, introduced a bill to extinguish all previous local laws and regulations "concerning the sale, distribution, use or display of tobacco products."

When health advocates drew the media's attention to the bill, there was confusion over who had initiated it. Bruno was quoted as stating that Pataki had requested the bill. The Pataki administration demurred. A Bruno spokesperson ultimately claimed that some senators had requested the bill's introduction, but he refused to reveal who they were. Due partly to its late introduction and the controversy whipped up by health and consumer groups, the Legislature adjourned without taking action on the measure.

After the tobacco industry documents came to Horner's attention in 1998, NYPIRG, Common Cause/New York, and the League of Women Voters of New York State filed a complaint with the New York Temporary State Commission on Lobbying about illegal gift giving by the tobacco industry's lobbyists. The commission investigated and found that the Tobacco Institute had indeed failed to disclose its expenditures. Lawyers for the Tobacco Institute admitted that it had spent $443,072 on lobbying in New York State in 1995 that it did not report, and that it had funneled those funds largely to the New York Tavern and Restaurant Association to advocate on its behalf before state and local governments.

In July 1999, the *New York Times*, basing an article on additional documents from the Philip Morris document archive, revealed that from 1995 through 1997, the tobacco giant had spent tens of thousands of dollars on gifts for Albany lawmakers. The *Times*'s examination of Philip Morris lobbyist Sharon Portnoy's credit card receipts, on which she had recorded the names of her guests, showed that at least 115 current and former legislators of the then 211-member New York State Legislature had accepted gifts from Philip Morris, ranging from meals at fine restaurants to seats at the men's finals of the United States Open tennis tournament, hotel accommodations, and tickets to the Indianapolis 500 and Yankees and Mets games. I was not among those so feted.

Interestingly, the *Times*'s coverage of the growing scandal also revealed that in 1995, Philip Morris contributed $10,000 to the Hungarian-American Chamber of Commerce, shortly before it underwrote the cost of Governor Pataki's trip to Hungary. The cigarette company dispatched lobbyist Tina Walls to dine with him and others in Budapest, though the Governor denied knowing anything about the company's contribution.

Philip Morris was fined $75,000 by the state's temporary lobbying commission for its failure to disclose its lobbying activities as required by law. Portnoy was fined $15,000 for her role. She was banned from lobbying in the state for the next three years.

In the end, in 2000, the Legislature and Governor parried over bills to ban members from accepting any and all gifts from lobbyists, but parrying was as far as it went.

Even so, the protracted Big Tobacco lobbying scandal was beneficial in that it neutralized the tobacco industry's efforts to roll back health legislation, and once the scandal had pierced broad public consciousness, a flurry of tobacco-related laws passed in Albany, including raising the cigarette tax, setting fire safety standards for cigarette manufacturers, and extending the indoor smoking ban. The reason, wrote Horner and Stern, was that the Legislature now needed to demonstrate to the public that it was not in the industry's pocket.

It took a similar public scandal for the Legislature in 2004 to finally eliminate a policy that effectively granted most state employees immunity from investigation when they leave the state payroll. This was passed at Pataki's beckoning. Until then, any employee who stole money or steered contracts couldn't be prosecuted under the ethics code, because as soon as the employee came under investigation, he or she could quit, and state officials could no longer pursue the matter. The catalyzing situation involved the resignation in 2004 of a state university college president—to deal with family matters, she explained at the time, though the Albany *Times Union* and the *New York Times* reported that she might have faced a state ethics inquiry into accusations that she allegedly offered to nudge a campus construction contract into the lap of a developer, who in return would pay to endow a university professorship that she herself could take over once she left her job as college president. The allegation was denied by her lawyer and never proven. But it appeared that her resignation effectively shut down the investigation.

Consider, too, Albany's secretive, backroom government from yet another perspective—that of the relatively open State Department of Transportation, as reported in June 2005 by the New York *Daily News*'s Greg B. Smith.

From June 2003 to June 2005 in that department alone, "lobbyists schmoozed the agency on nearly $1.3 billion in contracts," Smith reported. Smith obtained DOT records through the Freedom of Information law.

He discovered that "only a handful" of these contracts were awarded competitively with sealed bids, a process that significantly restricts influence peddling. Rather, nearly all the contracts—for everything from monitoring bicycle traffic to painting bridges to producing economic and demographic forecasts—were "negotiated," which allowed lobbyists to influence who won.

It wasn't until after the article appeared that the powers that be in Albany agreed—reluctantly, be assured of that—to require lobbyists to register and report any activity relating to winning contracts for clients. Up until then, the requirement applied only to lobbyists' efforts to influence the Legislature.

Probably no account of life in Albany would be complete without the abysmal intern-sex scandal that roiled the Capitol in spring 2004, a year that would mark the twentieth consecutive late passage of the state budget and be distinguished by such paramount legislation as a bill to let dry cleaners keep clothing left behind by customers for more than six months.

I had seen the fraternizing between some legislators and some of the 150 or so college students interning for State Assembly and Senate members and had frowned on it. For not only the Albany political culture but the social one, too, struck me at times as unseemly. In such a context, the $800,000-a-year legislative internship program for college students learning about government should have included rules or restrictions on sexual contact and special protections against improper sexual advances. It did not. Albany County district attorney Paul Clyne was so disturbed by the improper fraternizing that he actually advised that parents steer their college-age children clear of Albany—advice the *New York Times* would echo that May in an editorial, saying the students deserved a safer and more wholesome environment.

"Any father," Clyne memorably told the *Post*'s Fred Dicker, "who would let his daughter be an intern in the State Legislature should have his head examined. . . . I'm not going to call the place a cesspool, but I can say there is a group of legislators who, quite honestly, are here to get paid $80,000 a year and party three nights a week and who don't contribute anything to the process. . . . Everyone knows that for some people, legislators and some of the other staff people in the Legislature, the constant flow of young women in and out of the Legislature is viewed as an opportunity for them. . . . Lots of legislators feel that carousing is the main part of their job."

Clyne's comments weren't made in a vacuum. In 2002, in one of the more heavily covered incidents of its type during my tenure, Assembly Speaker Silver's then chief counsel, Michael Boxley, was removed from the statehouse in handcuffs on charges of having sexually assaulted a twenty-two-year-old woman who worked on the Assembly staff. A similar date rape accusation had been made against Boxley by another young staffer in 2001, but that woman didn't file a criminal complaint. The second woman did. And the year following his arrest, Boxley pleaded guilty to one misdemeanor count of sexual misconduct, admitting he had engaged in sexual intercourse with the woman at her apartment without her consent. He was fined $1,000 and placed on probation for six years, as well as on the state's sex offender registry. Under the guilty plea, prosecutors dismissed four felony rape charges against him. In March 2006, the Appellate Division of the Supreme Court reinstated Boxley because he had fulfilled the provisions of his sentence.

The Assembly's institutional response was to modify its sexual harassment policies and require that all verified complaints of harassment be kept on file for seven years. In early 2006, the Speaker's office agreed to pay $500,000 in public funds to settle a lawsuit brought by the victim, bringing the matter to a close—while, for me and others, bringing a further reminder that Albany remains a broken place, one that robs the state of a hopeful future.

At times, even the most insignificant perquisites, such as the right to pay comp time to legislative staffers, are fodder for abuse. It is "well known in legislative circles," Assemblyman Tom Kirwan of Newburgh told the New York *Daily News* in 2005, that legislative staffers are paid to perform campaign-related activities. Since using taxpayer funds to pay for reelection efforts is illegal, the payments are recorded as "comp time" earned for extra hours put in on regular constituent duties at a legislator's office. At one point, Assemblyman Kirwan had a simple solution to curb the routine abuse: pay the workers cash for overtime, no comp time allowed. Legislative leaders denied that any abuses occurred, however, and have not sought to tamper with a practice that, like politically based redistricting once every ten years, benefits the perpetuation of incumbency and the leadership's grip on power.

Albany, to be sure, is not a place for idealists.

CHAPTER 6

The Overcoat
Development Corporation

"Taxes," Justice Oliver Wendell Holmes Jr. memorably declared in one of his Supreme Court decisions, "are what we pay for civilized society." True enough—except that elected officials are wary of levying or raising taxes, lest we find ourselves voted out of office.

More than seventy-five years ago, New York State pioneered an ingenious mechanism to pay for the vast infrastructure of roads, bridges, tunnels, airports, and public transit needed to get millions of people to work and home again each day, without officially and directly placing the burden of constructing and maintaining these facilities on taxpayers' shoulders. That mechanism is called the public authority, a nonprofit corporation, owned and operated by state, regional, or local government, and funded by issuing tax-free bonds on a scale of tens or hundreds of millions of dollars.

Public authorities are attractive to voters and politicians alike because everyone gets to eat cake and have it, too. Bond buyers pay for construction and maintenance; the bonds are paid off with tolls and other fees collected from those who use the facilities. No one raises or pays extra taxes. It's all neat, simple, and clean.

Or so the authorities and the public officials who create them would like taxpayers to believe.

But just as there is no such thing as a free lunch (as both economists and fiscal conservatives are fond of reminding us), the proliferation of public authorities in New York State threatens to sink us under an avalanche of debt, which most taxpayers are unaware that they are morally obligated to make good on.

In February 2004, after I decided to leave the State Senate, state comptroller Alan Hevesi began calling attention to this political/fiscal nightmare. One of the comptroller's duties is monitoring the performance of state agencies and public authorities. His job is to make sure that the authorities comply with state laws regarding contracting and personnel practices, and that their expenditures are prudent and aboveboard.

To do this, the comptroller's staff periodically conducts audits that focus on selected programs and projects, checking items such as how well contractors fulfill their contracts, whether projects come in on time and on budget, and whether there are sufficient internal controls to prevent fraud and corruption.

The operative word about these audits is *periodically*. Another word is *narrow*.

When Hevesi began to highlight the state's looming "authorities problem," as his predecessor H. Carl McCall had also often done, he and his staff counted 640 of them. The number has since been revised upward to 733. Later he said the figure could be higher, but he didn't have the staff or budget to look into it. Coupled with the sheer size of many of the authorities, in terms of personnel and programs, not to mention annual ex-

penditures, the comptroller's office simply does not have sufficient staff to conduct thorough annual audits of each public
authority. Hevesi pledged that in an effort to provide greater
oversight, his office would increase its annual auditing to
cover three dozen of the state's public authorities—which
amounts to 6 percent of the total. (One observer estimated that
a battalion-sized team of auditors would be required to under-
take annual audits of each authority.)

Consequently, reviews conducted by the comptroller's office
usually focus on only a segment of an authority's operations,
and only a handful of public authorities are annually subjected
to audits.

Legislative oversight has been extremely weak, to the point
of being nonexistent for entire sessions. The Senate and Assembly each have committees with oversight power to investigate public authorities. I served as a member of the Senate's
Committee on Corporations, Authorities, and Commissions
during my first term in Albany, and can attest that its activities
were more akin to those of a worn-out rubber stamp than to
what an alert watchdog would do.

As a member of the Democratic minority, I had virtually no
say on any matter that came before the committee. It was the
chairman and his chief of staff who prepared the agenda and
consulted with Bruno and Bruno's top assistants to line up the
votes beforehand on what almost always proved to be innocuous issues.

That no major issues ever came before the committee for
discussion, much less inquiry or investigation, meant that the
vast majority of its members, Republicans and Democrats
alike, never attended its meetings. As was the way of Albany,
they proxied their votes beforehand to ensure Bruno had the
votes they needed to pass (or stifle) any measures they wished

to. A session's worth of such meetings threatened to lull me into a coma, and at the end of my second term in Albany, I decided to drop that committee and apply my time and energy to another committee that showed some potential for actually having some positive effect on the public good.

Little did I know at the time that the role and impact of public authorities on state government and state spending would explode as a major issue in 2005, a few months after I retired from the Senate. Since then, the relatively new chair of the committee, Republican state senator Vincent Leibel, has responded to some of these growing concerns, together with three Democrats, namely, Comptroller Hevesi, Assemblyman Richard Brodsky, and Attorney General Eliot Spitzer. Brodsky had been focusing attention on their concerns and the lack of oversight accorded public authorities for quite some time.

Indeed, Brodsky's work as chair of his chamber's Committee on Corporations, Authorities, and Commissions is an example, however rare, of how legislative oversight works when it is allowed to do so. In October 2003, hearings conducted by his committee revealed that staff members of the state's Canal Corporation, a subsidiary of the New York State Thruway Authority, had engaged in bid rigging to steer rights to develop land along the canals' right of way for a ludicrously paltry sum of money.

In theory, oversight by the state comptroller and the Legislature should be a formality, since each public authority is governed by a board composed of private citizens who are appointed to represent and safeguard the public's interest in the management of their authorities' programs. The Governor nominates these public members, and for the most part they are formally appointed with the Senate's consent and receive no salary for the services they render. Their primary task as public members is to set goals and policies for how their authority accomplishes its tasks and to review how those goals and policies are implemented.

The Canal Corporation scandal revealed, however, a number of weaknesses in this public-member governance model. First, unlike directors of private-sector corporations, board members of public authorities receive no compensation for the hours they put in. Therefore, of necessity, they serve on a part-time basis. Moreover, their part-time attention to governance issues may be further diluted by serving on the board of one of the authority's subsidiaries.

Indeed, one factor in the origin of the Canal Corporation scandal was, as one member of its board later acknowledged, that the board spent 90 percent of its time on Thruway Authority matters and only 10 percent on Canal Corporation affairs.

A second weakness in the authority governance model is that because they serve on a part-time basis, board members depend on the authority's staff to provide accurate information upon which to make decisions about policies and programs. When the staff is determined to cover up activities such as favoritism and corruption that are at odds with the public's interests, it is possible to keep such embarrassing—not to mention possibly illegal—activities buried for years.

As reconstructed by Attorney General Spitzer and Inspector General Jill Konviser-Levine, the seeds of the scandal were sown in 1992, when control of the state's canal system was transferred from the state's Department of Transportation, whose operating costs are appropriated annually from tax revenues, to the New York State Canal Corporation. Under this new arrangement, the cost of running the canals was shifted from the state budget's balance sheets to those of the Canal

Corporation's parent, the Thruway Authority. That move amounted to fiscal sleight of hand. While it allowed the Governor and Legislature to claim that New York's taxpayers were being relieved of the cost burden of operating the canals—since the money to do so would no longer have to be appropriated each year as part of the state budget—the burden simply popped up on the books of the Thruway Authority, whose budget is also paid for by taxpayers, albeit indirectly in the form of toll revenues paid when driving on the thruway.

Shifting responsibility for operating the canals to another arm of the state was merely cosmetic. Doing so didn't address, much less solve, the fact that the canal system was a money loser: it cost roughly $70 million to operate annually, but took in less than $2 million in users' tolls and fees. The authority was faced with the problem of absorbing those increased operating expenses while still meeting its fixed expenses of repaying bondholders.

In September 1995, the authority approved a plan to generate revenue that it expected would help defray this added expense: areas along the canal system would be opened to residential and commercial development. Rights would be sold to entrepreneurs who would create canal-side communities featuring upscale homes and boat marinas. Eight months later, in May 1996, the Canal Corporation's chairman sent a letter to some two hundred companies and individuals, soliciting possible participation in developing the canal.

Richard Hutchens, who eventually won the Canal Corporation's approval to proceed with such development, did not appear on the initial solicitation list. His name was added after he contacted Donald Hutton, the Thruway Authority's deputy director of planning. Though he had no direct experience in developing canal-side properties—other than as a manual laborer during the 1940s for an uncle who developed a community near Orlando, Florida, and as a foreman in the 1950s at a drainage canal construction site at an Air Force base in Texas—Hutchens quickly emerged as the Canal Corporation staff's favored candidate.

As Spitzer and Konviser-Levine detailed in their seventy-five-page investigation report, which partly relied on Hevesi's fiscal oversight work, during the next three and a half years Canal Corporation staff members failed to perform due-diligence background checks that would have revealed Hutchens's nonexistent qualifications for the project; routinely passed along, and sometimes embroidered, Hutchens's renditions of his qualifications; and made few, if any, efforts to check whether similar canal communities existed (they did), in order to determine an accurate fair-market price for the rights Hutchens sought. Hutchens failed to inform the corporation board that he had defaulted on a riverboat tourism project for which he had no experience, but which the staff rigged so that Hutchens was presented as the sole viable bidder. The board staff members steered Hutchens to lobbyists for the purpose of influencing corporation board members to approve Hutchens's proposal after some board members expressed doubts and tabled consideration of it, and the staff placed him in contact with campaign fund-raisers who solicited donations for Governor Pataki. The staff also misled board members about precise details of Hutchens's development proposal.

At several points during the course of Hutchens's negotiations, Nancy Carey, one of the three Thruway Authority public members who served on the Canal Corporation's three-person board, raised questions or objections that momentarily derailed the deal. A daughter of former Governor Carey, who was appointed in 1993 by her father's successor Mario Cuomo,

Carey was relied upon by her colleagues for her expertise as a partner in a commercial real estate development firm when land development proposals were brought to the Canal Corporation. Therefore, in late 1997, when Carey expressed her concern that the corporation was undervaluing the development rights it was being asked to sell to Hutchens, the deal ground to a halt. But only briefly.

Rather than compelling Hutchens and the Canal Corporation staff to draw up a more financially feasible proposal, Nancy Carey's objections served to goad the staff into (1) advising Hutchens to buy political influence by making a contribution to a state official whose campaign manager happened to have taken a leave of absence as the Canal Corporation's director of operations, and (2) engaging a lobbyist to meet with Carey in December 1998, in an attempt to overcome her objections. To her credit Carey, however, remained unconvinced about the financial arrangements, and a decision was again postponed.

Nonetheless, in the end Hutchens—with the complicity of the Canal Corporation's staff—got what he wanted: exclusive rights to develop all of the Canal Corporation's developable land along the canal for the fire-sale price of $30,000. On January 27, 2000, the corporation board approved handing over development rights to Hutchens—who immediately started renegotiating the terms of a formal contract, again with covert assistance from corporation staff.

The final contract, signed by Thruway Authority representatives in December 2001, contained provisions favorable to Hutchens that had never been presented to, much less approved by, the corporation board. The final, failed links that allowed the deal to blossom into a scandal were approvals of the contract made by the Office of the State Attorney General and the Office of the State Comptroller, in January and May 2002, respectively. It took Brodsky's oversight hearings to air the irregularities involved in the Hutchens deal and to put an end to it. In the process, New Yorkers were afforded a glimpse into the problems we now confront for having abdicated our authority for controlling the state's finances and development.

The explosive growth of public authorities as a tool to manage all varieties of what were once functions of state and local government, and therefore subject to voter oversight, is a comparatively recent development.

New York's pioneering public authority was actually a cooperative venture with its neighboring state New Jersey. The Port Authority of New York and New Jersey was established in 1921 to develop shipping and rail facilities in the two states' common harbor area at the mouth of the Hudson River. Proponents of the project came up with the public authority model as a way to insulate harbor development from the vagaries of state legislative budgeting and appropriations processes. Efforts of such enormous size had in the past frequently foundered or suffered long delays when recessions, depressions, and cost overruns threatened to outstrip legislatures' abilities to raise sufficient revenues to proceed on an annual pay-as-you-go basis. And the harbor project was so large and was expected to take so long to complete that the legislatures of both states surrendered their direct say as a way to avoid straining their states' annual budgets.

It was in the 1930s, in the depth of the Great Depression, that Robert Moses put public authorities on New York State's map. Hailed at the time as "the man who can get things done" without falling prey to the pitfalls of fraud, inefficiency, and waste that Tammany Hall's political patronage demands had imposed on previous public works projects, Moses engineered the consent of beleaguered state and local officials to create authorities as a means of capturing tens of millions of dollars in federal appropriations intended to provide employment and restart the nation's stalled economy. Using federal funds as start-up capital, Moses's authorities then raised additional funds on the bond market. Banks and other financial institutions willingly bought authority bonds because Moses's projects were self-financing: highways, bridges, and tunnels that charged users tolls and fees, which were earmarked for maintenance and paying off bondholder debt. New York State and New York City, limited by their constitution and charter, respectively, regarding the amount of debt they could accumulate, and severely constrained in the amount of revenue they could raise from taxpayers reeling from the Depression, viewed Moses as a miracle worker and, until the 1960s, rarely challenged his suggestions for creating yet more authorities to tackle yet more massive job-producing public works projects.

By 1956, with prosperity returned, New York legislators decided to assess the number and scope of the state's authorities as part of a review of state government activities. The Hults Commission, formally known as the Temporary State Commission on Coordination of State Activities, identified fifty-six authorities and recommended the elimination of twenty. However, the state's creation of authorities was only temporarily abated. During the 1960s, authorities proliferated, mainly to establish financing for housing and urban development projects without having to go to the voters with statewide referendums that asked taxpayers whether they consented to assuming the cost burdens of the projects.

With the state having found a way around the prospect of taxpayer revolts by technically keeping this form of financing from showing up on the state's budget ledger, even more authorities have been created since the 1970s, mainly for the purpose of issuing debt for state and local government projects and services. By 1996, when a State Commission on Government Integrity was appointed to review Albany's operations, state officials had lost count of the number of authorities. In "Underground Government: A Preliminary Report on Authorities and Other Public Corporations," the panel acknowledged, in tones of exasperation rarely vented in such documents: "At present, so far as Commission staff has been able to determine, no one has even an approximate count of how many of these organizations exist, where they are, much less an accounting of what they do." (In a footnote, however, the report cited a 1985 *Local Government Handbook,* published by the Governor's office, that cited 46 statewide or regional authorities, and "about" 529 local authorities.)

A cherished example of New York State's crazed addiction to creating public authorities at the slightest provocation is the Overcoat Development Corporation. Established in 1986 in an attempt to encourage an Indiana clothing manufacturer to relocate its operations to the Mohawk Valley town of Amsterdam, the corporation has led a mysterious existence. Several years ago a *New York Times* reporter attempted to uncover what success, if any, this rather specialized authority had achieved, and went to 633 Third Avenue, in Manhattan, its address of record. No "Overcoat Development Corp." was listed in the lobby's directory of the building's tenants, and no one in the building could be found who had ever heard of it. But as of February 2005, when Comptroller Hevesi enumerated at least 733 existing authorities, the Overcoat Development Corporation was still listed among them, as a subsidiary of the Empire State Development Corporation mega-authority.

It is easy to deride the "overcoat authority" as an example of Albany's infatuation with authorities. But to dismiss the resort to authorities as a mere foible runs the risk of failing to understand that reliance on authorities is an admission on the part of state officials that the very functioning of state government has long been deeply dysfunctional in meeting its most elemental responsibility, which is sound fiscal management.

The Local Government Assistance Corporation is a case in point.

LGAC was created in June 1990, with authority to issue up to $4.7 billion in bonds, whose debt service costs are covered by appropriations provided by one-quarter of the state's 4.5 percent tax levied on all sales transactions. The reason for LGAC's creation, as stated in its "Annual Report for Fiscal Year Ended March 31, 2004," is a fine example of bureaucratic obfuscation:

> LGAC was created as an integral part of an overall program of State fiscal reform to eliminate the State's practice of financing substantial amounts of local assistance payments during the first quarter of the State's fiscal year through the issuance of short-term tax and revenue anticipation notes (the "Spring Borrowing"). LGAC bonds were issued for the purpose of making payments to local governments and school districts in a manner that provides such funds to such entities than had been the State's traditional practice.

In order to properly decode LGAC's account of its creation and raison d'être, a reader needs to be aware of the most outstanding symptom of state government dysfunction, which until April 2005 had plagued Albany for two decades: inability to pass a state budget by the constitutionally mandated date of April 1.

These perennially late budget agreements meant that no one in Albany could authorize release of state revenues to local governments and school districts for social service programs and education. There was a constant threat that lack of a budget agreement in Albany would choke off the flow of funds, and that the local programs New York's citizens relied on would grind to a halt.

Rather than solving its dysfunctional ways head on, Albany resorted to a quick fix. Instead of letting everything grind to a halt while the Legislature and Governor dithered and dickered, they agreed on a system whereby the state would be allowed to take short-term loans from banks and other sources, and these loans would then be used to tide over local governments and school districts until a budget was passed. These loans were secured by promising to pay back the borrowed money—with interest, of course—from the proceeds of future tax collections (the "short-term tax and revenue anticipation notes" cited above). Since New York State's budget is supposed to be agreed upon in early spring, and because it wasn't for twenty years, and because the state had to borrow funds to keep the state's local government and education machinery in motion, this became known as the "Spring Borrowing."

But a quick fix for one dysfunction soon led to another dysfunction: the Spring Borrowing unavoidably drove up the cost of state government, which meant higher taxes for state residents. Rather than fixing the budget process, Albany resorted to another quick fix: creating yet another public authority— the Local Government Assistance Corporation—with the power to issue bonds and notes up to $4.7 billion. Now the eyesore of those "Spring Borrowing" short-term tax and revenue anticipation notes disappeared from the state's budget ledger, and the cost of repaying the LGAC's bonds and notes was buried in internal transfers from the state's sales tax collections to the LGAC. Albany's inability to pass a budget on time continued to exact a toll on taxpayers—except this time, as in a game of three-card monte, the aim of the game was to make it harder for taxpayers to put a finger on why they kept losing their money.

The LGAC has had its defenders, and sometimes in unexpected places. Writing in a January 1998 paper issued by the Manhattan Institute, ordinarily a politically conservative scourge of New York State and New York City mismanagement follies, William J. Stern and Edwin Rubenstein noted, "Admittedly, the LGAC is a regrettable expedient, made necessary by the irresponsibility of leaders in Albany. But given the political reality of New York, such borrowing is a reasonable way to ensure that the state's residents are not forced to endure regular interruptions in basic services. Moreover . . . LGAC bonds account for only a small fraction of overall state indebtedness."

True. Yet the Local Government Assistance Corporation exists only because our Legislature and Governor have not found the means to properly do the jobs for which they were elected. The losers are the New Yorkers who elected them and whose taxes continue to be diverted to fund an authority whose ultimate, if unintended, function is to permit the state's elected officials to grandstand each year over the state's budget, and to insulate them from being held accountable for the consequences of their grandstanding.

On paper and in theory, the New York State Constitution invests the power of the purse in those who pay the taxes that give the state money to spend on services for its residents. And it provides a safeguard to prevent state officials from spending wildly without taxpayer approval. If state officials want to go into debt to pay for a project that can't immediately be paid for out of current or prudently anticipated revenues, and if they want to pay off that debt by adding to the taxes that New Yorkers already pay, then state officials have to give voters an opportunity to vote yea or nay about whether they're willing to pay more taxes for the project. That's called a general-obligation debt referendum, and as can be extrapolated from the fact that New York residents are among the most heavily taxed in the nation, obtaining voter approval in such referendums is a notoriously iffy proposition.

Creating a public authority is a way Albany gets to raise and spend taxpayer money—more than $20 billion a year—without being required to ask taxpayers whether they want to pay higher taxes. That's because, in theory, public authorities pay for their projects by selling bonds to bond holders, and then paying back those bonds with revenue produced by the project. In the midst of the Great Depression, Robert Moses demonstrated that this proposition worked with the bridges and tunnels his authorities built. In fact, revenues from tolls were so much greater than originally projected that, had he been so inclined, he could have paid off debts to bondholders years before the bonds were due to mature. But few New Yorkers at the time cared: the tolls taxpayers paid seemed reasonable, bondholders were happy, and no one's state taxes were raised.

Today, however, the Moses-model public authority doesn't describe the vast majority of the 733 (by last count) authorities. Many of the authorities established since the 1960s don't generate steady streams of revenue from their projects. Since bondholders want some sort of security that their bonds will be paid back, the state of New York provides that guarantee. But

since the state can't guarantee that, as a last resort, it will pay
off the bonds from general-obligation tax revenues without
first obtaining voter consent, most authority bonds are backed
by the state's moral obligation to pay off the bonds if the authority fails to do so.   :

Though "moral obligation" sounds like a weak and perhaps
weasel-worded guarantee, state officials familiar with the cir-
cumstances surrounding the near failure in 1975 of the Urban
Development Corporation—a New York State public authority financed by billions of dollars in bond borrowing—are unlikely to forget the havoc moral obligation can wreak on those
who would take it lightly. The UDC's near collapse coincided
with a recession-softened dip in the real estate market that
threatened to push New York City over the brink of fiscal in-
solvency and into bankruptcy and default on its city-issued
bonds. When the federal government balked at providing loan
guarantees to tide the city over its threatened default, the state
was called upon to step up to the plate with assistance.

The only source of funds to meet these twin threats was private money markets, and the price was steep. Funds were made
available, but interest rates to service the debts—paid out of
state taxpayers' pockets—skyrocketed. Had the UDC been financed through general-obligation debt, the state's taxpayers
would have had a collective choice whether or not to vote on
raising their taxes to pay for its projects. As it was, the UDC's
creation as a public authority robbed them of that choice, and
they paid anyway—and at higher-than-anticipated rates once
the prospect of default became real. (Part of the procedure
that staved off UDC's default was to subsume it as a subsidiary
of, yes, yet another authority, the Empire State Development
Corporation, created to take over UDC's obligations and debt.)

The UDC debacle, and New York State's near collapse in its

wake, were memorable and cautionary events for public officials who picked up the pieces and set the state's fiscal house in order. But memories fade with time, and with renewed prosperity Albany has gone on a spending spree fueled by proliferation of public authorities with authority to borrow money—without voter approval—by issuing moral obligation bonds.

The State Comptroller's Office reported in February 2005 that New York's public authorities held approximately $70 billion in debt—up from approximately $41 billion only seven years earlier. Moreover, of that $70 billion, more than half—$43 billion—represented borrowing on behalf of the state government.

Further, in order to service the debt on that $43 billion, the state was shelling out $3.3 billion in 2004–2005, an amount projected to rise to $5.1 billion by 2009–2010. All of this debt, and the annual payments necessary to service it, has been racked up without the state's voters having been given a chance to approve whether they agreed to take on the "moral obligation" that accompanied this accumulation of debt.

A telling example of how New York's public authorities have been subverted to respond to political demands rather than to the public interest is the rise and demise in 2005 of New York City mayor Michael Bloomberg's plan to build a 75,000-seat football stadium on Manhattan's West Side.

Bloomberg, throughout the first term of his mayoralty, boosted the idea of a stadium proposal as a project that would repatriate the New York Jets professional football team from neighboring New Jersey and at the same time stimulate building on the West Side by bringing thousands of construction and service jobs to the city. He also touted the project as a central venue for the 2012 Summer Olympic Games, until the International Olympic Committee, in July 2005, chose to award the games to London.

At first the stadium project's anticipated costs were pegged at $1.4 billion, but they rose to $1.7 billion and then $2 billion before settling in at $2.2 billion. The mayor and Governor Pataki made equal pledges of $300 million in city and state funds to underwrite the project, with the state's share to come from the Empire State Development Corporation. Securing the state's $300 million proved to be the stadium's Achilles' heel, although this did not become apparent until very late in the game.

Opposition to the stadium by citizens' groups, which feared traffic congestion, pollution, and construction-related disruption, as well as skepticism voiced by good-government organizations about job creation and other purported economic benefits that stadium advocates said would follow in the project's wake, made no dent in the mayor's and Governor's determination to see the stadium built. Their confidence in their ability to prevail was based, in large measure, on their belief that they could bypass both the city and state legislatures and finance the measure through the state's public authorities. Of course, this meant there would be no public referendum. Such confidence represents a remarkable demonstration of the extent to which the state's public authorities, originally designed to act as nonpoliticized tools of the public's interests, have become unilateral tools of politicians.

Moses, the legendary public servant who made public authorities the way to "get things done" when it came to public works projects between the 1920s and the 1960s, was notoriously haughty in his dealings with elected officials, and more often than not they were forced into the role of supplicants who begged for his attention and largesse. The state, however, no longer has a public works czar—in part due to elected officials' determination never again to suffer the humiliations Moses imposed on their predecessors. Public authorities' chairpersons and boards are now more responsive when the Governor makes his wishes known, since it is the Governor who has the principal role in appointing them to their posts. Moreover, the longer a Governor serves, authorities grow increasingly likely to bow to the Governor's wishes, since the Governor will have had a hand in appointing increasing percentages of the chairs and boards of all the state's authorities. At that point, there is a risk that an authority's decisions will no longer be based on rational, dispassionate, nonpolitical assessments of the public's interests, but on the political calculations of the person who appointed a majority of its board. That dynamic flies in the face of the reason why states and municipalities supposedly establish public authorities in the first place: to insulate decisions about massive public works spending and indebtedness from political calculation and interference.

The stadium proposal, which gathered momentum throughout 2004, hinged during 2005 on how much money the Metropolitan Transportation Authority would ask from the football team's owners as the price for selling development rights to construct a stadium on the site of the authority's West Side railway yard facility. Initially, the Jets offered $100 million. This soon rose to $210 million after critics of the MTA, which had recently announced its intention to reduce services on the city's subway system in response to a projected budget deficit, charged that the authority was acting in a fiscally irresponsible manner by offering the site at a fire-sale price. Research into the MTA's records subsequently uncovered an internal report showing that the authority's property appraisal staff had estimated the value of the site's development rights to be $923 million.

The MTA, not quite recovered from revelations two years earlier that its board had, in effect, been keeping two sets of accounting ledgers—one showing an operating deficit, which it used when attempting to justify fare increases for the city's subway and bus lines, and another, internal set, which showed that the authority's fiscal position was not nearly so dire as publicly proclaimed—reconsidered its asking price for development rights to its West Side yards. The Jets subsequently raised their offer to $250 million.

Additional pressure descended on the MTA when Cablevision, a Long Island–based company that owns Madison Square Garden, offered $400 million for the rail yards' development rights. Cablevision said it intended to use the site to build a residential complex of 5,800 new moderate-income apartments, which, the company projected, would create 3,200 construction jobs over twelve years and generate $100 million in state and city taxes by 2012. Supporters of the stadium contended that the cable operator's proposal was a cynical ruse designed to thwart competition for sports revenue, which Cablevision feared would be drawn away from Madison Square Garden, where their New York Rangers and New York Knicks professional hockey and basketball teams, respectively, play. Yet another company, Transgas, entered the fray, offering the MTA $700 million for the development rights, in return for the authority's promise to support its plan to build a power plant in Brooklyn and to purchase its power for twenty years.

On March 31, the MTA board announced its decision: it accepted the Jets' offer of $250 million, to be paid in five $50 million installments over four years—or $210 million in a lump sum. Authority officials justified their decision by citing the football team's pledge to pursue an accelerated construction schedule and its commitment to hire minority- and woman-owned businesses as subcontractors. MTA board member John Banks told the *Daily News*, "All of that equals greater than $400 million [the total offered by Cablevision]." Transgas's offer was reportedly rejected on grounds that its bid had been accompanied by extraneous and burdensome conditions.

The MTA's decision momentarily buoyed Bloomberg's and Pataki's hopes, but a final hurdle still had to be cleared: approval by a crucial but relatively little-known state agency called the Public Authorities Control Board.

The PACB was created in 1976, in the wake of the Urban Development Corporation's near bankruptcy, "to receive applications for approval of the financing and construction of any project proposed" by any of eleven of New York's public authorities, including the Empire State Development Corporation, successor to the UDC. Technically, the PACB consists of five members, each appointed by one of Albany's main legislative fixtures: the Governor, the Senate Majority Leader, the Assembly Speaker, and the Minority Leaders of each chamber of the Legislature. But in true Albany fashion, only representatives of the Governor, the Senate Majority Leader, and the Assembly Speaker are empowered to cast votes; representatives of the Senate and Assembly minorities can listen and ask questions but cannot vote on items that come before the board. Strip away the camouflage of its nonvoting members, and the PACB is yet another iteration of New York's perennial rule of "three men in a room." And because the PACB requires a unanimous vote for any request to pass, gaining approval of any measure offers maximum leverage for horse-trading among Albany's triumvirate—another subversion of the original aim of creating public authorities in order to insulate decisions about massively expensive public works projects from political pressure.

Thus, it was a disagreement among the triumvirate—Pataki, Bruno, and Silver, with the latter two abstaining—that prevented a unanimous vote to approve the Empire State Development Corporation's expenditure of $300 million in state funding for construction of a West Side stadium. When the PACB met on June 6, 2005, to consider the ESDC's request, the Governor's representative voted in favor, and Bruno's and Silver's representatives were instructed to abstain—which had the same effect as casting a negative vote. Though Bruno did not explicitly state a reason for his vote, he was reported to have been seeking an equal $300 million in funds for economic development projects in areas outside of New York City, especially upstate. Silver was more direct, stating his belief that the stadium would draw funds and future economic development from lower Manhattan and reconstruction of the World Trade Center site destroyed in the 9/11 terrorist attack—a site that happens to be in the electoral district Silver represents in the State Assembly.

It is impossible to determine how much revenue New York State and New York City might have realized had the stadium proposal been approved. All the projections offered—by the football team as well as by various elected officials who supported the project—were fuzzy to begin with. The out-of-pocket cost to state and city taxpayers, however, can be calculated with greater accuracy: $300 million in ESDC funding for the stadium, $300 million from the ESDC for Bruno's wish list, $300 million in city commitments, and another $673 million, representing the difference between the $923 million at which the MTA's appraisers valued development rights to the West Side rail yards site and the $250 million for which the MTA board agreed to sell those rights to the Jets football team. That total comes to $1.573 billion of public funds financed through New York State's public authorities—$1.573 billion of public funds upon whose expenditure state and city officials assiduously tried to make sure taxpayers would not have an opportunity to vote, whether or not they thought a football stadium was how they wanted to spend their taxes.

It almost goes without saying these days that the prospect of a new stadium needing an obscure state board's approval was first and foremost a windfall for lobbyists for the New York Jets and the Cablevision media giant of Long Island.

But while it was an extremely important matter at that moment in New York's struggle to regain its footing in the wake of September 11, 2001, the question of the stadium, and the broader economic considerations also at issue, occasioned remarkably little involvement by the 210 other legislators in Albany. The Majority Leader, the Speaker, and the Governor were the ultimate audience for the blizzard of lobbying—a record, in fact—for television ads and direct cajoling, along with additional courting efforts by Bloomberg.

Long before the stadium came before the obscure Public Authorities Control Board, Pataki and Bruno had tended to send their representatives in their stead to its brief monthly meetings, which are held in an unmarked room in the State Capitol. The board, in turn, seemed to do little to keep in check the large grouping of authorities under its fiduciary purview.

That two men who abstain from casting votes can determine so much in so little time without public hearings or expert testimony about the potentially enormous implications of a historic land-use decision speaks volumes about the need to restore democracy to Albany.

•   •   •

It was said of the Bourbon kings that, individually and collectively, they neither forgot anything nor learned anything, which contributed to their demise as the most prominent reigning family of Europe. Albany's "three men in a room"—and their successors—may well share the Bourbons' fate should they continue to avoid facing the fiscal threat posed by reliance on public authorities to finance the state's debts.

The few measures Albany has adopted to address its unabated abuse of public authorities amount to halfhearted half-steps. Late in June 2005, in the wake of scandals at the Canal Corporation, the MTA, and other authorities, the Legislature authorized appointment of an inspector general and creation of a separate budget office to provide oversight of the authorities' operations, and the Governor created a Commission on Public Authorities Reform, chaired by Ira Millstein. As might be expected, Albany's major actors hailed these moves as significant steps on the road toward redemption. Assemblyman Richard Brodsky, who brought the canal scandal to light, proclaimed, with a generous dollop of hyperbole, "We have recaptured these Soviet-style bureaucracies." Outside the confines of the statehouse, however, longtime observers remained skeptical, noting that the Governor, who appoints members of public authorities' boards, would now also appoint both the inspector general and the chief of the new budget office charged with riding herd over . . . his appointees.

Nor has Albany confronted its addiction to fiscal legerdemain. Rather, it has continued to pile yet more debt onto the books of the state's public authorities in order to produce, in 2006, a record $112 billion budget; declare a $2–4.5 billion revenue surplus; give New York City some $11.2 billion to construct and refurbish its schools; *and* justify a round of tax cuts for the state's wealthiest taxpayers just in time for legislators to ask voters to reelect them come November. To work these miracles, New York's Dormitory Authority (whose purview was long ago broadened to finance construction of hospitals) will be authorized to issue $2.6 billion in bonds for the city's school projects. Another $9.4 billion for capital construction will be raised by the state's guarantee to back debt issued by city-controlled public authorities.

As it now stands, according to a report published in April 2006 by the Citizens Budget Commission, New York State's public authorities are responsible for $227 billion in debt—slightly more than twice the size of the year's budget. Of that, only $56 billion—one quarter of the total—will be repaid through revenues generated by the authorities, such as tolls and other usage fees. Another $40 billion is to be repaid by universities and hospitals that have availed themselves of funding through the Dormitory and other authorities. The remainder, $187 billion, is to be paid off from state and local government revenues—another, politer, and less-threatening-to-voters way of saying "taxes."

Or perhaps, when the bill comes due, Albany will once again attempt to resort to what it has done with increasing frequency during the past fifty years: authorize its public authorities to go even deeper into debt by issuing still more bonds designed to pay off New York State's off-the-books debt in an evermore desperate attempt to delude taxpayers into believing that—really, truly, trust me—there *is* such a thing as a free lunch.

Ultimately, the state's runaway public authorities must be severely restricted in number and powers, and the state comptroller must be given the staff and resources needed to audit their functions. As Hevesi put it in late 2005, according to an account by Michael Gormley of the Associated Press: "Public authorities are an immense shadow government that have offered continuous and unambiguous proof of the truism that when no one is watching, the increase in mismanagement and corruption is dramatic. It is absolutely absurd that these public authorities are still not answerable to any public body."

CHAPTER 7

The Money Pit

In November 2000, a small group of Democratic State Assembly members, concerned about the fertile ground for financial mischief in Albany, announced at a press conference that they had traced numerous state grants to a variety of hidden accounts in the New York State budget. The legislators called these murky accounts "slush funds," and they were collectively worth hundreds of millions of dollars. They existed under the virtually exclusive control of Albany's top two legislative leaders and the Governor, noted the lawmakers.

The first of the funding items they described was the Community Facilities Enhancement Program. This program, which sounded so very official, was begun as a $425 million appropriation in the 1997–98 state budget.

While it was known that the appropriation was designed to help finance new sports stadiums across the state, such as a $93 million arena for Buffalo, and that the Governor, Assembly Speaker, and Senate Majority Leader contributed equally to the full $425 million amount, additional projects subsidized from this pot were never identified within the budget. Any fair and complete reckoning of how or whether all of this appropriation was used, and what happened to any unspent balance, became one of those enduring and commonplace mysteries that often characterize the budgeting of billions of dollars of public funds in New York State.

It is also an example of the business-as-usual fiscal practices that would never pass muster in any respectable company or any self-respecting, professionally staffed state legislature around the country. New York, after all, has arguably the nation's heaviest tax burden; inordinately high and rising debt; and late budgets in twenty of the last twenty-two years. The entire state budget, which totaled more than $105 billion by 2005, and $112 billion in 2006, is so huge and approximate that few elected representatives ever bother to ask too many questions about appropriations, or try to find out whether and how the money is to be spent. Under the master/serf dynamic that exists in the Legislature in Albany, most lawmakers seem to recognize that such conduct would be construed by their house leadership as rebellious if not out-and-out dangerous, and thus it could jeopardize their status in a tight party hierarchy.

When one lawmaker did ask such questions loudly, as Brooklyn Democratic assemblyman James Brennan did in issuing, with others, the so-called slush fund critique, the answers that came from the top were less than satisfying or complete. Brennan, as a result of his perfectly legitimate and understandably daggered questions about the use of the public's money, began to encounter barriers to advancement in the Legislature.

There was more to his report. The other "major slush fund" Brennan's group traced was known as the "Education Lump." The 1999–2000 state budget contained two such education lump-sum appropriations, which totaled $27 million. Listed as "grants-in-aid," they did not specify the recipients. "Behind the scenes," Brennan stated, "the legislative leaders choose which projects get funded."

While Brennan was not saying that tax money was being pocketed, he assailed the murkiness surrounding so many millions of dollars budgeted in accordance with accounting "principles" that were not worthy of a state legislature. The vagueness increased the possibility of favoritism, conflict of interest, or even outright theft of public money.

Just consider pensions, as E. J. McMahon and the Empire Center for New York State Policy did in July 2005, when it issued one of a regular series of red-flag reports of a sort that come and go in New York, too often unread and all but ignored. The research center's study began by noting that sky-high state retirement costs were straining state and therefore county budgets, to which many kinds of costs were shifted, with more than $4 billion in pension enhancements added to the state's retirement costs since 2000 alone.

The Legislature's 2005 response to what many argue are deep-seated structural issues—pension costs have risen faster than even the costs for the state's $45 billion Medicaid program, the state's largest single expense—was the passage of hundreds of measures designed to increase pensions for unions and workers whose financial support and votes they count on.

The dependable generosity, which was driven by election-year dynamics and obscured by the close-to-the-vest manner in which the state budget is cobbled together once a year (with its predictable coda of closed-door negotiations among the three top leaders), burdens both the state's finances and those of county governments, whose revenues contribute to the overall $120 billion public employee pension investment fund.

Should the state government be handling the enormous

pension funds differently? That's hard to say, in part because the tightly controlled, undemocratic process of passing a budget or doing just about anything of consequence in the Capitol doesn't allow time on the floor or in committees for public debate or expert input. Yet there are few topics more complex, financially fraught, or worthy of open discussion and vigorous debate than the subject of public pensions.

Because of the way the budget is hashed out in Albany, access is often the thing that matters most. It trumps argument almost every time.

The gradual cultivation of favors resulting in a backroom deal is the currency in Albany, as much now as ever, and probably more so. Common Cause's New York City–based director, Rachel Leon, has noted that many of the lobbyists hired by the gambling industry in the state were former power brokers in state politics, people such as Patricia Lynch, the former chief of staff to Assembly Speaker Sheldon Silver; Bill Paxon, a former New York congressman, now a partner in a Washington law firm whose clients include the Seneca Nation of Indians; and Bill Powers, the former head of the state Republican Party. They provide access to key decision makers for those wealthy enough to afford them.

John O'Mara, according to Common Cause, is a good example of how average citizens and their elected representatives can be cast to the winds compared to those with personal ties to the Big Three. O'Mara is the former chairman of the New York State Public Service Commission, which oversees the placement of power plants and other state energy matters. He served on Governor Pataki's campaign and transition teams. Pataki appointed him to the state Public Service Commission.

O'Mara later became a lobbyist on behalf of energy giant

Niagara Mohawk. Fine. But as he lobbied legislators for the power corporation, he continued to serve as the Governor's lead negotiator with Indian tribes and chaired Pataki's advisory council on federal judgeships. "No wonder he's called the 'ultimate insider,' " wrote Common Cause, discussing how power companies have sought to stave off grassroots pressure to close down old plants and reduce toxic emissions.

One could spend a great deal of time, as Common Cause's Rachel Leon admirably does, trying to connect all these dots, to show cause and effect. It is a necessary but difficult chore, due to the many ways that those in power have connived and conspired over the years to safeguard it. Even high court decisions fail to get in the way of their budget gamesmanship.

In fact, New York is a state where even a landmark ruling on education funding by its highest court, the Court of Appeals, can go virtually ignored. The ruling in favor of the grassroots Campaign for Fiscal Equity required the state to come back to the court with a formula for funding public schools that did not shortchange New York City and other low-income urban school districts, those with the highest proportion of economically and educationally disadvantaged students.

As much as $30 billion is supposed to flow to city schools over five years due to the court's 2005 decision. But the Governor chose to appeal the court decision, a process that probably will not be resolved until he is out of office. This would leave in place a school funding process that all but guarantees unequal school funding between cities and suburbs, in violation of the court's interpretation of the state constitution and in particular its requirement that every child is entitled to a "sound, basic education." The needed legislative debate on where the money will come from and how it will be used has never happened. This item was not even considered in the 2005 budget.

Why this is so has to do with the Governor's enormous clout over the budget and, it turned out, his political goals. Pataki, who had appealed and reappealed the court ruling to no avail, announced in August 2005 that he would not seek a fourth term after public opinion polls suggested the principal Democratic challenger, Eliot Spitzer, might beat him. So it was clearly easier for the Governor to brush off the enormously important, expensive, and controversial school funding issue—as did Bruno, whose political base is not in New York City—than to hew to the spirit if not the letter of the court decision. The Campaign for Fiscal Equity will undoubtedly return to court as soon as necessary to demand a legislative response.

In the arena of education and in many others, Silver and Bruno frequently contend that they are up against an extraordinarily powerful executive branch and thus their own sway is limited. This is true. Unfortunately, though, their contention is that they cannot therefore abide too much independence of action or thought by their legislative members so that they can show the Governor a united front as often as possible.

The truth is that legislators can't serve their constituents adequately or fairly by acting as leadership's pawns or puppets. Nor does their fawning subservience necessarily strengthen their leaders' hand in annual budget negotiations with the Governor. My view is that it would be better for the citizenry to have strong and empowered representatives. It would also be better for their leaders. I can, for example, envision a legislative leader in such an environment using the threat of breakaway factions within his own party as a tool with which to negotiate with the Governor over the budget.

"Governor, I'd like to give you that $1.5 billion highway widening grant," an Assembly Speaker might be able to credibly say, "but I'm not going to be able to sell that one to my New

York City members, and I want to keep my job, thank you very much. So how about some additional mass transit aid to keep them happy? Then we can talk about your upstate highways."

In the meantime, the leader will have gotten better advice, a broader and perhaps more complex sense of the considerations and interests at issue, from a more active and representative lot of lawmakers. If the price of that is more contentiousness in his body, well, we live in a democracy, don't we?

It's curious: a November 2005 referendum asked voters to give the Legislature greater power over the budget than it currently has vis-à-vis the Governor. The notion had some merit but was defeated. But if the objective was to give the people more say through their elected representatives, that won't happen. If the referendum had been approved, the result would have been to give additional power to only two of the three men in the room. At least now the third man, the Governor, a statewide official, can be voted out of office. It is virtually impossible for voters to punish the well-insulated Senate Majority Leader and Assembly Speaker, or even remove one of their Senate or Assembly minions. Furthermore, the Governor is elected by those among the 19 million people of New York who can or bother to vote, while the Senate Majority Leader is elected by 310,000 people and the Assembly Speaker by 125,000 people.

If a choice has to be made between whether the Governor or the Legislature should control the budget introduction and approval process, then the Governor should continue to have more power then the Legislature. The Legislature simply cannot be trusted, due to structural lack of accountability to the public and lack of transparency in the way it raises and spends the taxpayers' dollars it controls.

In 1927, the citizens of New York State amended their constitution to implement what is called the "executive budgeting system," an overhaul of the way New York was governed and the way in which the budget was put together. The system imposed new responsibilities on the Governor to ensure that there was at least one person in the process who was accountable to voters statewide. It gave the Governor what was thought to be a reasonable degree of clout to be effective, and it has been the subject of court decisions over the decades.

"The Governor is the constructor or the architect of the budget," said Brian Stenson, deputy director of the Rockefeller Institute, during a 2005 forum on state government. "The Legislature is the critic. Under the Constitution, the Legislature has budgetary authority to only approve an appropriation in its entirety; delete an appropriation in its entirety; reduce the amount of an appropriation without changing the when/how/where conditions on how that money is to be spent; or it can add a new separate item of appropriation subject to gubernatorial veto.

"What it can't do," Stenson continued, "is substitute its judgment for the Governor's. It cannot delete the Governor's appropriation for X, vote that down, and then conjure up its own version and put it in place. As long as legislation is related to the appropriation, the Governor can condition the appropriation on the legislation. In other words, the Governor could for instance add language to a Medicaid appropriation bill. He could appropriate X number of dollars and put a line in there to say, 'None of these dollars are to be used for abortion.'

"The Legislature's option then would be to accept the appropriation with the limiting language, or reject the entire appropriation and shut down Medicaid. Those are the only two options. . . . That leaves the Legislature with the power to create chaos, to do nothing—to refuse to pass the Governor's budget, to leave things hanging, and hopefully induce him by political pressure to negotiate. That's really the check and balance on the Governor's power."

Clearly, then, the Governor holds the big cards.

The U.S. Congress hasn't followed the same path. Checks and balances are not simply a theory in Washington. There are lengthy hearings and debate each year on the federal budget, despite the fact that the White House has enormous clout. And there is an independent General Accounting Office to examine how costly programs in federal agencies are operating, and how far reality is from legislative goals and intent. Albany has none of this.

Citing the way legislators are shut out of the budget and lawmaking processes may sound like sour grapes from a former minority Democrat in a Republican-majority house, and if that were all it was, it would be easy enough to dismiss. But only by considering the self-serving, internal logic of Albany can one even begin to understand how badly things work there—or how, to name one big example, a $45 billion program to provide health care to the poorest New Yorkers is barely scrutinized by the State Legislature, year after year.

It's true. Medicaid, the forty-year-old legacy of Lyndon Johnson's Great Society, has made itself a barn-sized target for unscrupulous people in the medical industry in New York, partly because the Pataki administration, in its cocooned wisdom, provided just fifty civil servants and a few outside contractors to investigate recipients of Medicaid funds. One of the prices paid for chopping down government's role was a diminution in the public regulatory and watchdog apparatus to keep track of government spending.

"It's like a honey pot," a former senior Medicaid prosecutor in Albany who retired in 2003 told the *New York Times* in its scathing, two-part exposé by reporters Clifford Levy and Michael Luo, which appeared in July 2005. The articles estimated that Medicaid fraud in New York State could amount to billions of dollars.

It should come as little surprise that some opportunistic New Yorkers in the medical industry realized they could act with relative impunity to tap into Medicaid's federal, state, and city billions—including dental and medical clinics, hospitals, transportation services, and pharmaceutical enterprises.

Several other states' health departments have anti-fraud offices that are larger than New York's in proportion to the size of their Medicaid budgets, the *Times* pointed out. So New York's 301 employees in anti-fraud efforts recovered less than half as much money from Medicaid fraud prosecution as those in Texas, Florida, and New Jersey. Of those 301, only 50 were fully dedicated to anti-fraud work, as noted above. The rest shared that task with other jobs, such as administrative duties.

"The decline of fraud control in New York," the second of the two *Times* articles said, "contrasts sharply with the situation in other states. In 1998, California, which had several high-profile Medicaid fraud cases in the 1990's, added about 400 employees to an existing staff of about 40 charged with rooting out abuse. The number of fraud cases referred to prosecutors has since doubled."

The *Times* caught many Albany regulars by surprise, including key members of the Governor's staff and the legislative leaders as well. There had been no probing hearings during my tenure on Medicaid spending. Comptroller Alan Hevesi, like his predecessor H. Carl McCall, wasn't ever invited to testify on the issue. A see-no-evil, hear-no-evil posture was the norm, and that was nothing new. An earlier comptroller, Erie County Republican Ned Regan, once reported that during his fourteen years as the state's chief financial officer no legislative committee asked him to testify on any topic, much less so important a one, despite his repeated offers to do so.

Pataki may have assumed that Medicaid has such a strong liberal constituency, and there were so many financial interests invested in its bloated condition, that no one would bother to look closely at its enormous price tag, at least for the remainder of his time in office. In addition, as with the Court of Appeals decision requiring fairer formulas for state education aid, Pataki resolved that Medicaid was one hornet's nest he didn't want to poke into. The Governor said nothing about lack of oversight prior to the exposé. When the exposé was published, though, he marshaled his underlings for a hasty press conference and announced an increase in oversight staff.

The Assembly Speaker and Senate Majority Leader had little to say about the Medicaid system too, having failed to charge a committee with taking up the issue of Medicaid oversight in a serious and committed way, though it was quite clear that the more than 4.2 million poor people who depended on Medicaid would be helped if fraud and waste were reduced, including those tens of thousands of illegal claims for reimbursement that were approved. Since the state's legislative and executive branches preferred to operate without independent oversight, it isn't all that much of a stretch to say that independent review of the state Health Department was just as unwelcome. Nor do the legislative leaders want a separate entity of any kind to help determine how much money will be available for spending on any big-ticket budget line in the next year—as many states allow. Rather, the Big Three want to retain the power to argue and deal among themselves.

Don't even think about long-term financial planning, which an independent budget office, such as the one New York City voters created in the late 1980s, or a variation on the General Accounting Office as it exists in Congress could provide. The Albany triumvirate doesn't want anyone looking over its shoulder. It has never even agreed to establish a four-year financial plan, another basic facet of how other states or any enterprise manages its books.

New York State does not conform to generally accepted accounting principles. It runs on a cash-based system worthy of a Prohibition speakeasy or a nineteenth-century political machine.

In response to public indignation, the 2005 and 2006 budgets were passed on time, albeit with strong criticism of their substance from major newspapers and fiscal watchdogs. And it's important to remember that it was all done through secretive negotiations and that the legislators' reforms were illusions. The Governor and legislative leaders managed to pass the 2005 budget on time only by hoisting up an incomplete one, leaving for future discussion an estimated $1.7 billion in state funds to help the homeless, acquire land for environmental protection, close landfills, beautify parklands, invest in construction projects planned for public and private colleges, and repair the state's broken-down voting system—the latter a federally funded mandate. These were dropped from the budget to get it signed on time. Furthermore, the federal government is now suing the State of New York, which it claims has done the worst job in the nation of improving its election system.

Bruno and Silver also acceded to $350 million in so-called anti-terrorism projects sponsored by Pataki as part of their last-minute maneuvers. This measure was tucked inside $40 billion in budget bills that passed both houses, the *Daily News* reported on March 30, 2005, though some legislators, such as

Assemblyman Bill Parment, a Democrat from Jamestown, called the anti-terror projects a "slush fund." "Our procurement process is already a sieve," he said.

Assembly Speaker Silver acknowledged Parment's criticism, apparently happy to divert attention from the unusual efforts to fast-track the budget to Pataki's boondoggle projects. "We have to go with what we have to go with," he told the newspaper. "Is it wrong? Absolutely. I agree with him 100 percent."

TV news in those heady weeks had us glimpsing three men negotiating, sometimes heatedly, along with their loyal deputies—a photo op designed to give the impression of glasnost having finally arrived in the corridors of the Capitol. But in the end, the budget at the center of the flurry of activity wasn't a completed budget at all. Democratic senator Eric Schneiderman, who graded the process an "F-minus," said, "Everyone is already gushing in pride. But I don't think passing one on-time budget automatically turns us into golden boys."

Former Governor Mario Cuomo agreed. "It's not a real budget if, when the Legislature adopts it, they know there are a billion and more dollars they have to add to it to meet their important needs," Cuomo told the *New York Times*. "It sounds to me like a facade of a budget—it looks like a budget, but it's not a budget."

Some of the real unanswered questions were: Where was the money in the 2005 budget actually going? What were the state departments of health, education, and transportation planning to do with their shares? Will all contracts with the state be conducted by an open bidding process? Who will write the new legislation? Will the money be well spent? There is no way to know.

The state attorney general, Eliot Spitzer, had an equally caustic reaction when I spoke with him soon after the celebrations. Spitzer, a national figure as a result of having clamped down on the illegal practices of corporate America, post-Enron, was getting ready to run for Governor of the state.

"The late-night final budget approved by the State Legislature late last night and early this morning does not fundamentally change the process that existed in the past," he said. "They used a Governor's 'message of necessity' "—an executive-branch hammer meant for emergency situations only—"to cut down the three-day period when budget proposals are voted on by the Legislature to within twenty-four hours. It was used throughout the night, thereby preventing legislators from understanding what was taking place and what the bills actually said."

Spitzer noted many tough decisions were postponed until the middle of April 2005 or later, or never, as far as anyone knew for sure at the time; the bare-bones budget was passed at the April 1 deadline. "Three men went into a closed room to make the tough decisions without telling their colleagues what they had done until they had to vote on thousands of pages in a few hours," he said.

"And how does one constrain health care spending?" Spitzer went on, seemingly thinking aloud, though in a calculated way, too, as he was about to embark on the biggest election contest of his life. "This is a very, very serious problem. There was ignorance by members, when they voted to complete the budget process, of how much it would cost and where the money would come from. This finalization of the budget was an absolute victory for the status quo over any type of reform," Spitzer added. "We are now back to what existed before."

Spitzer is not alone in urging the establishment of a general accounting office—a truly independent agency monitoring the state budget process and following up on how public money is spent, as New York City has had since its city charter was amended by voters in 1989. Sadly, under a newly approved "independent" budget office for the state's annual operating budget, the budget-monitoring unit is to be under the ultimate control of the Governor. So it won't be objective at all.

The Legislature also passed a bill in 2005 to intensify oversight of the scandal-plagued public authorities and their multibillion-dollar operations. It voted to create a new Inspector General with jurisdiction over the authorities and an Authority Budget Office to review authority budgets. Sounded good for the TV sound bite. But the oversight entities, if they actually come to pass under the Pataki administration, will not be independent. Rather, the legislation allows for the entities to be appointed and controlled by the executive branch.

In September 2004, the Brookings Institution issued a study of income and poverty data for upstate New York. The study found that personal income upstate grew at just half the national rate in the 1990s and by 2000 trailed the country by 11 percent; more than half of its meager income growth was the result of increases in government transfer payments from Social Security, Medicare and Medicaid, and the Earned Income Tax Credit.

On an hourly basis, the study found, upstate New York's workers earned lower wages than their counterparts by age, race, sex, and educational attainment nationwide. Its highest-income households earn substantially less than the national average. Its lowest-income households saw little earnings growth in the 1990s.

I mention that study—one of several depicting the economically sluggish state of affairs in much of New York State's rural communities and old industrial centers—because some sources believe that several Albany lawmakers are determined to soon vote to raise their own annual pay to more than $100,000. A raise requires approval in two consecutive legislative sessions. Politically speaking, it usually requires a fig leaf or two. These sources believe that the strategy could be to link the pay hike for elected lawmakers to perhaps more raises for judges. Other sources do not believe this to be accurate. Only time will tell.

Gratified by the generous raise and stipends, the impulse for independence of mind, exploration, and dissent, so critical in a democracy and the life of a troubled state, will be buried even more in our State Legislature.

Finally, from the halls of the Empire State's executive branch came surreptitiously recorded conversations. The subject matter relates to a valuable coin for any Governor, whether Democrat or Republican—and that is patronage.

While the conversations may or may not have been illegally tapped, in any case they landed in the lap of Fred Dicker of the *New York Post* in August 2005. Gossip they may be, but they are of genuine significance because New York is a state, like most, where the public gets only glimpses of their leaders speaking at carefully staged and controlled settings. In this instance, Thomas Doherty, one of Pataki's top aides in his first term, and various other people close to the Governor were captured in private chats on Doherty's line. The snippets, while incomplete, should remind voters that the government needs to be more transparent and accountable, with democracy up and down the line.

In regard to patronage, a voice on the tapes, recorded shortly after Pataki won office in 1994, is that of Alfonse D'Amato, Pataki's kingmaker and then a U.S. senator from New York.

Doherty described his difficulties placing a Republican patron in a $60,000-a-year Department of Motor Vehicles job. A less than enthusiastic official with DMV had told Doherty that the requested appointment would be a "heavy lift."

"Did you ask him how the hell he got his job?" D'Amato reportedly said, supportively, to Doherty. Doherty said he responded to the DMV official at the time, "Oh yeah? Well, just make sure it gets f—ing done!"

"I laughed at that point," Doherty went on to D'Amato, describing his reaction to the official's recalcitrance.

Pataki's response to the *Post* report was to call angrily for a federal inquiry into the unknown source of the recordings. On the matters of patronage, the doling out of jobs to political allies, and the involvement of a top aide and a U.S. senator who was his patron, Pataki of course said nothing.

What should be discussed, but hasn't been, was "that the Pataki crowd has used Albany as its personal hiring hall," as a *Times* editorial properly noted in its Sunday Long Island section on August 28, 2005.

CHAPTER 8

Restoring Democracy

Sometimes Albany's corruptions warrant jail terms. Sometimes they are difficult to discern, as when officials pull strings to endeavor to ensure that big political contributors receive lucrative state contracts. Small matters, such as the abuse of comp time by legislative staffers, are left as business as usual, too minor for prosecutors to bother with. Large ones sometimes attract headlines, as they should, and outrage often ensues. Sadly, it rarely results in serious reform.

While no regulations or government framework will ever be able to prevent corrupt individuals from stealing from the public purse, much more could be done to constrain the almost unbridled power of personal ties and big money to Albany's Big Three and their many supplicants.

Why, one should ask, is there no truly independent budget office as in New York City or Washington, or public authorities watchdog, or autonomous and empowered executive and legislative ethics commissions to keep a sharp eye on the government?

The state's leaders have not seen fit to create a climate of transparency and oversight. When such monitoring mechanisms nominally exist, they have not provided them with the legal and financial means to weed out criminal and unethical behavior. As just one example, the Legislature's ethics commission, in fact, is but a "temporary" panel. Its chairman, though admirably aggressive, lacks subpoena power, significant budgetary support, and a truly nonpartisan staff.

As I look back, my years in the New York State Legislature were very disturbing, especially after I got to know how the place takes care of its own and blindsides the voters. I've concluded that only top-to-bottom reform can bring a semblance of democratic rule to Albany.

Moreover, it has become clear to me upon further reading, interviews, and reflection that fundamental change requires many reforms of both the executive and legislative branches, and decentralization of the enormous power now held by two top legislative leaders, whoever they happen to be at any given time, and without regard to their particular political affiliation.

What could result, I believe, are much more dynamic and accountable Senate and Assembly members, freed to dissent if necessary from their leadership and do battle on behalf of statewide interests as well as their individual districts and constituencies.

A path to anarchy and gubernatorial checkmate, as some contend?

Hardly.

Decentralizing the all-controlling power wielded by two legislative leaders is the surest way toward a stronger, more vibrant, and truly representative Legislature. The shackles and strictures of lockstep leadership control that characterize Albany stymie debate and innovation, as well as public interest in what goes on in Albany. It also leads to self-inflicted paralysis, year after year.

Legislators stand little chance of being unseated, even when targeted. But by 2004 I reached the point of no return, after nearly nine years in office, and said goodbye to my generous pay and perquisites, staff assistants, and public attention. But it didn't seem right to simply wash my hands of the place. I decided to add my voice to all those committed men and women throughout the state now clamoring for change.

Hence, for whatever good it might achieve, this book.

The NYU Brennan Center's state-by-state comparative analysis of the New York State Legislature in 2004 recommended that the Senate and Assembly leaders take it upon themselves to improve their procedures and make them more democratic. To their everlasting credit, twenty-seven Democratic Assembly members signed a resolution in support of many of the reforms proposed in the study.

There is no doubt in my mind of the importance of many of the Brennan Center's recommendations, and in fact, at least for starters, the two bodies did somewhat amend their rules the following year. However, the new rules ended up leaving even more power in the hands of the Majority Leaders, especially in the Senate. The reforms were piecemeal, timid, and often counterproductive. Legislators were in the same disempowered condition in which I had found them. Their reluctance to institute genuine democratization should demonstrate once and for all that the Legislature and executive branch will not and cannot reform themselves. They will not voluntarily make Albany more democratic, more open to public scrutiny, and fundamentally more accountable to the voters, unless compelled to from the outside.

Consider changes brought after the Brennan Center report. The Senate amended the body's operating rules to permit, not forbid, secret votes on motions, and to cease recording votes on motions and amendments brought by individual senators on the floor of the Senate.

The Senate also passed a rule that, in effect, institutionalized absentee voting and forbade any senator to force a vote on a bill in committee or bring resolutions to change rules on the floor.

Under the mantle of reform, the Senate decreed that such resolutions must be submitted to the Rules Committee, which is controlled by the Majority Leader. The Assembly rules change did require members to attend sessions and even some meetings, something that led to much grumbling among many of its pampered minions.

But the Assembly would go only just so far on its own, with the Senate digging in its heels and undercutting demands for openness and collaboration. The Speaker no doubt feared he would be left at a tactical disadvantage compared to the Majority Leader if he went too far in the direction of democratization. Policy decisions continued to be made by the Speaker's staff in the closed-door confines of the office. Conference committees, where differences that exist between Senate and Assembly bills are ironed out, remained rare. There was, in short, little improvement.

Radical surgery, a constitutional convention, is necessary. I believe that a constitutional convention, which would throw open the entire system of governance to reexamination, is the most important place to begin.

As we've seen, legislative leaders' dabbling with rule changes will never amount to much, even in an atmosphere of public indignation, nor will the success of any one party's gaining control of both houses or changing leaders result in the kind of fundamental reordering that is required.

Additionally, the Governor and Legislature's reluctance or inability to heed the state Court of Appeals ruling in the Campaign for Fiscal Equity education case suggests the limits of going to the courts to bring about change to legislative processes.

The voters themselves have a great responsibility. Yet apart from professional good-government lobbies and myriad advocacy organizations devoted to specific causes, only a relative handful of the state's citizens appear to know or care about what goes on in the state capital. Yet care they must. For what happens in Albany affects every man, woman, and child in the Empire State.

And how about the voting booth—isn't that the path of last resort in a democracy? The problem is, it's not really a democracy we live in, and district lines, among other things, have been rigged to prevent competitive elections and protect incumbents; the New York State Legislature has one of the lowest turnovers of any legislature in the nation.

Certainly, one of the roots of the Albany mess is the disproportionate influence of campaign contributions. While the Legislature did in 2005 require—for the very first time—that those who lobby state agencies disclose who their clients are, the moneyed interests that hire lobbyists are still able to unduly influence the political process because the state's campaign finance laws are lax and poorly enforced compared to those of New York City and the federal government. Many elections in the state are underwritten by large contributions from a well-defined and limited number of wealthy, connected individuals and special interests.

Reporter Michael Cooper wrote in the *Times* in June 2005 that so-called soft-money contributions, which have been banned by the federal government, inundate state campaigns—sometimes in $100,000 installments. These nearly unlimited contributions are made to the innocuously named "housekeeping accounts" of political party organizations.

Unrestrained soft-money contributions also help parties protect incumbents who face strong challengers, in much the same way that legislative leaders use hundreds of thousands of dollars in discretionary public funds, known as member items, to ease incumbents over the top in potentially close races. They also carve out odd-shaped districts in the service of protecting or enhancing their party's control of their house.

The New York State Commission on Government Integrity pointed out the campaign finance loopholes and laxity in its much-publicized reports on city and state government less than two decades ago. But it takes a three-way agreement in Albany to change self-serving campaign finance laws. Therefore, they have been left undisturbed.

"First," the commission recommended, "New York State's existing campaign finance laws are wholly inadequate to disclose and monitor, much less to limit, contributions to powerful legislators or legislative races by moneyed interest groups. "Second, interest group money plays an undesirably significant role in legislative campaign fundraising, particularly for party committees and individual legislators."

Just as fundamental as campaign finance reform, there is a critical need to introduce a nonpartisan redistricting process, to prevent the parties from tailoring district lines to suit their political needs. Many states, notably Iowa, have taken up this reform, but not New York. The point of redistricting as practiced in New York is not, as stipulated by law, to seek to ensure that minority voters retain influence as voters even as demographics shift, as recorded every ten years by the Census Bureau.

"The legislature's redistricting task force is armed with detailed data on population and voting characteristics that allow it to tailor a district to an incumbent's needs with block-by-block precision," wrote Mark Berkey-Gerard in an article in the online *Gotham Gazette.* "They are drawn to favor the majority party and ensure that each majority incumbent gets reelected." The New York Public Interest Research Group has wryly noted that districts often resemble coffee stains on a map or bugs squashed on a windshield.

Albany also needs to do away with its shadow government, by which some $30 billion in tax-exempt financing is awarded annually. The sprawl of state authorities—public benefit corporations acting independently of the admittedly flawed process by which money is raised and spent by the Legislature—operate with little scrutiny. What exactly does each of them do? How do they operate? Why so many? Who gets hired to run them? On what basis? Who scrutinizes their day-to-day activities? One is hard-pressed to find the answers to such questions, given the blanket of secrecy and lack of oversight under which they function.

These entities are generally exempt from what little controls exist in the legislative and executive branches to limit favoritism, influence peddling, fraud, and waste. They are also exempt from civil service requirements and from many restrictions on how contracts are awarded, auditing and financial reporting requirements, and conflict-of-interest rules.

Not only authorities but also the Legislature, state agencies, and the Governor's office harbor great potential for malfeasance, mismanagement, and conflicts of interest. They are all the focus of the law firms, bond underwriters, banks, engineering firms, contractors, and consultants—many of them former state employees—that interact with them. So mechanisms such as tough laws and ethical codes need to be put in place to rein in and make accountable the many governmental branches and offshoots.

Term limits are both one of the most controversial and one of the most popular policies in the country. A recent poll commissioned by the Empire Center for New York State Policy found that approximately two-thirds of New Yorkers would look favorably upon term limits.

Between 1990 and 2000 voters backed term limits for state legislatures in twenty-two states by an average popular margin of two to one. They have already gone into effect in about fifteen states and more are expected. Nebraska voted for term limits three times between 1992 and 2000, persisting when their first two attempts were overruled by state and federal courts. Now their objective will be realized.

Unfortunately, in most states, it is difficult to get rid of incumbents any other way because of gerrymandering. Nebraska and other states that voted for term limits hope that it will lead to more "citizen legislators." A Nebraska official said that some of the state's veteran politicians have been playing golf with lobbyists for a generation. Interestingly, a few term-limited states such as Arizona and California have become more ethnically diverse, boasting greater numbers of Latinos. Arkansas and Michigan have had more African Americans; California can claim a dozen more women in the assembly since term limits started. The newcomers are also more suspicious of lobbyists than their predecessors. However, the longer they were legislators, the more they developed relationships with lobbyists.

New York City voters twice approved term limits in government in 2001, affecting the terms of office not only of City Council members but also of the mayor, public advocate, city comptroller, and borough presidents. I long opposed term limits in the Legislature, but I am of the revised opinion, based in part on the city's recent experience, that they have been relatively successful. When elected officials can serve twenty, thirty, or more years, as in Albany, they lose contact with reality and feel that they are part of a permanent elite. In the years since its inception in the city, new faces and new leadership have come into existence, and the City Council is at least as strong as the previous council, which was dominated by its Democratic Speaker. Fears of political chaos have not been realized. There is also no sign that special interests, wealthy contributors, and bureaucrats have gained the upper hand over temporary lawmakers—or that the council Speaker was enfeebled vis-à-vis the constitutionally more powerful mayor's office in the annual budget negotiations.

Then, too, New York State's term limits would not have to be exactly the same as New York City's. They can and probably should include staggered terms in order to prevent an almost complete turnover every eight years (and with it, the loss of a good deal of institutional knowledge all at once). It might also be better to have the terms for each legislator extending to a maximum of ten or twelve years. This could also make it easier to stagger their terms and give them time in office to accrue influence and accomplish things.

If a constitutional convention were held, many delegates would probably agree that state legislators should not be able to continue to hold an office for an open-ended period of time, as it is already too easy for them to turn their jobs into lifetime sinecures simply by serving the leadership in a submissive manner. And because the Governor is more accountable and given to turnover—serving longer than three times is almost unheard of in contemporary politics, as the voters inevitably want someone new—I don't feel a gubernatorial term limit is needed. Others may feel differently. New Jersey, for example, has a two-term limit for its Governor.

Standing in the way of any solutions to the crisis in Albany is the lack of a real Legislature, one that would be permitted to do all the things that many legislators have done for decades in Washington and in many states of the Union: debating and proposing and holding hearings. That kind of enlivened, representative body, to which the public is entitled and upon which a democracy depends, does not exist in Albany. It is an embarrassment and a shambles and, as I've said, it desperately needs to be overhauled.

The particular route of a constitutional convention is not recommended frivolously. I am well aware that a convention opens the entire state constitution—any part of it—to possible amendment by delegates elected by the people. Our current state constitution contains, for example, some of the best safety net protections for the poor of any state. But as we have seen with welfare policy, it's federal policy that determines the shape of state policies concerning poverty relief. Likewise, it's the U.S. Supreme Court, not the state constitution, that addresses such social issues as the legal right to abortion.

New York is one of fifteen states with mechanisms for calling a constitutional convention. The Legislature must pass a bill in two consecutive sessions, one of them before and the other after a particular year in which legislative elections are held. If approved in the two sessions, the question of holding a convention goes to the voters.

If voters then approve of holding a convention, delegates are subsequently elected by the voters (thus providing a reasonable opportunity for rank-and-file party members to consider the needed revisions). Whatever revisions to the constitution get approved by the delegates then go on the ballot for voters' final approval or rejection.

"I think it's a risk worth taking," said the hardworking and constructive Westchester Democratic assemblyman Richard Brodsky at a 2004 forum on Albany sponsored by the Rockefeller Institute. "I think the people of the state can be trusted to be fair and sensitive to a variety of needs." I agree.

Brodsky, who distinguished himself with his unusually aggressive review of some of the state's public authorities through widely covered public hearings in 2004, also wants serious consideration of a possible alternative to something as sweeping as a no-holds-barred constitutional convention: individual constitutional amendments adopted by the Legislature in two consecutive, separately elected legislative sessions and put to the voters for final approval.

Brodsky's wish to avoid a full-blown constitutional convention is understandable, but I don't believe it's possible. One can't trust the Legislature to create, via the constitutional amendment mechanism, a nonpartisan redistricting panel to strengthen ethics rules and enforcement, to curtail and abolish superfluous state authorities and their back-door borrowing, and to institute debt reform and budget reform. Any of these needed measures would dilute the power of the leadership of the Legislature, so don't look for them happening anytime soon.

Because there is a crisis of governance and of public confidence born of decades of institutional failure, only a bold remedy can possibly cure the patient. A constitutional convention is where New Yorkers must look for the serious changes needed to revitalize our governing institutions and state, and many, including former Governor Mario Cuomo, believe it's necessary to have a constitutional convention as soon as possible.

The state constitution itself gives the people the right to petition the Legislature for a statewide voter referendum on holding a constitutional convention. One can be convened at any time with voter approval of such a ballot referendum. Even so, every twenty years voters are automatically asked if a convention should be convened. "Shall there be a convention to revise the Constitution?" is the wording of a ballot measure voters will by law next see no later than 2017, twenty years after the majority of state voters said no to the question of holding a convention in 1997. Political leaders across the state, citizens of all political persuasions, and the media can exert influence—more readily and consequentially than many may think—toward convening a historic convention well *before* 2017.

Former state senator Richard Dollinger reminded me that I am hardly alone in my belief about the importance of a convention sooner rather than later. Dollinger, who was the county chairman for the Democratic Party organization in greater Rochester and recently became a judge, sees campaign finance reform as a linchpin if there is ever to be a reinvigoration of Albany, yet he believes it will probably never come about without constitutional amendment, whether by legislative means or by convention-approved referendum. He said the "signs of collapse" in the Capitol will create the conditions for something as dramatic as a constitutional convention.

Dollinger said he does not see either party restoring democracy on its own. "If the Democrats regain control of the Senate," he added, "the current processes would continue, except another party would simply be in charge."

So Dollinger calls for "an e-mail march on Albany," with people around the state, liberals and conservatives and independents, raising one million signatures via e-mail and delivering those petitions demanding a constitutional convention in order to start the process of real reform in Albany.

The state constitution has actually been substantially revised at least four times in New York history. The original was
drafted and approved even before the U.S. Constitution. The
major rewrites were in 1821 (when a Bill of Rights was in-
serted), 1846 (enshrining a referendum process for determining whether a new convention should be held every twenty
years), 1894 (establishing the right to an education for every
child in the state), and 1938 (providing for a social safety net,
public health programs, and labor and housing rights). It has
been amended more than two hundred times, either through a
constitutional convention or through legislative approval in
two consecutive sessions plus approval by the voters of a ballot
question on the suggested amendment.

Since 1960, at least ten states have adopted new constitu-
tions, while other states have substantially revised their consti-
tutions.

"Now what we want to have is a wide-open convention
that would take everything up: California-style ballot initia-
tives, campaign finance reform, term limits, and any other issues," said Dollinger. "The only way this can be done is
through a constitutional convention, because any legislator
who wants to remain in the Legislature and enjoy the power
and the perks will never vote for things the leadership doesn't
support."

As I see it, the statewide editorial-page outcry, the defeat or
near defeat of some incumbents, and the "Fix Albany" electoral
campaign may have been the opening shots in a movement for
reform. Public pressure needs to grow so that, at the very least,
the following vitally important changes can occur:

• Sweeping campaign finance reform—including subject-
ing legislative campaign committees to contribution limits of

$1,000 and prohibiting them from transferring funds to any other politician's campaigns.

- Term limits for all Assembly members and senators.
- Eliminate special budget allocations worked out among house leaders and the Governor for their special projects.
- Require total transparency of any and all member items, which are intended to serve community needs, not the electoral agenda of the house leaders.
- Set up a nonpartisan redistricting board, as the redistricting process is now used by Senate and Assembly leaders to prevent truly competitive elections and protect their house majorities.
- Establish a permanent, nonpartisan ethics commission to police the Legislature, executive branch, and state agencies.
- Limit the state to a maximum of at most a dozen public authorities at any one time, such as those responsible for highways and transit; scrap the rest and incorporate their functions into the state budget. At the same time, establish a nonpartisan commission, with an ample auditing staff, to oversee the public authorities and report on their activities and expenditures to the Legislature and public.
- In the Legislature, require seniority-based appointments of committee chairs, subject to party vote; this will give committees some autonomy from the house leader to devise and debate legislation.
- Equalize resources for staffs and services for every legislator, regardless of whether he or she is in the dominant or minority party in his or her respective house. This will prevent the second-class treatment of minority-party members in both houses and the denial of one-person, one-vote principles for their constituents.
- Require every bill voted out of legislative committee to be

voted on by the entire house, not selectively weeded out or junked by the house leader.

• Establish a mechanism to resolve legislative differences concerning bills passed in the Senate and the Assembly.

• Create another mechanism to resolve legislative differences in compatible bills passed in the Senate and the Assembly.

• Establish a nonpartisan, independent budget office to monitor the state budget and state finances, including debt accumulation and taxation.

There is much more that needs to be done.

Three Men in a Room should be viewed as part of the process of getting "we, the people," as well as our elected leaders, moving in a direction toward what is aptly described as a "grand conversation" on democracy and decision making in the Empire State.

New York needs to open up a closed governance system, bring in fresh ideas and new blood, and spread the sunshine and vitality of democracy across a state government that now stumbles about in near darkness.

SELECTED BIBLIOGRAPHY

Ackerman, Kenneth D. *Boss Tweed: The Rise and Fall of the Corrupt Pol Who Conceived the Soul of Modern New York.* Carroll and Graf, 2005.

Berle, Peter A.A. *Does the Citizen Stand a Chance?* Barron's Educational Series, Inc., 1974.

Benjamin, Gerald, and Richard Nathan. *Regionalism and Realism: A Study of Governments in the New York Metropolitan Area.* Brookings Institution Press, 2001.

Brands, H.W. *Theodore Roosevelt: The Last Romantic.* Basic Books, 1997.

Caro, Robert A. *The Power Broker: Robert Moses and the Fall of New York.* Knopf, 1974.

Connery, Robert H., and Gerald Benjamin, eds. *Governing New York State: The Rockefeller Years,* vol. 31, no. 3. The Academy of Political Science, 1974.

Connery, Robert H., and Gerald Benjamin, *Rockefeller of New York: Executive Power in the Statehouse.* Cornell University Press, 1979.

Cuomo, Mario. *Diaries of Mario Cuomo: The Campaign for Governor.* Random House, 1984.

Davis, Kenneth S. *FDR: The New York Years 1928–1933: A History.* Random House, 1985.

Desmond, James. *Rockefeller: A Political Biography.* Macmillan, 1964.

Ellis, David M., James A. Frost, Harold C. Syrett, and Harry F. Carman. *A History of New York State.* Cornell University Press, 1967.

Gallagher, Jay. *The Politics of Decline.* Whitson Publishing Co., 2005.

Greenwald, Richard A. *The Triangle Fire, The Protocols of Peace, and Industrial Democracy in Progressive Era New York.* Temple University Press, 2005.

Handlin, Oscar. *Al Smith and His America.* Little, Brown, 1958.

Hevesi, Alan G. *Legislative Politics in New York State: A Comparative Analysis.* Praeger, 1975.

Ingalls, Robert P. *Herbert H. Lehman and New York's Little New Deal.* New York University Press, 1975.

Josephson, Matthew, and Hannah Josephson. *Al Smith: Hero of the Cities.* Houghton Mifflin, 1969.

Kramer, Michael, and Sam Roberts. *"I Never Wanted to Be Vice-President of Anything": An Investigative Biography of Nelson Rockefeller.* Basic Books, 1976.

La Follette, Robert M. *La Follette's Autobiography: A Personal Narrative of Political Experiences.* University of Wisconsin Press, 1960.

―――. *Narrative of Political Experiences.* University of Wisconsin Press, 1960.

Martin, George. *CCB: The Life and Century of Charles C. Burlingham, New York's First Citizen 1858–1959.* Hill and Wang, 2005.

McElvaine, Robert S. *Mario Cuomo: A Biography.* Charles Scribner's Sons, 1988.

McEneny, John J. *Albany: Capital City on the Hudson: An Illustrated History.* Windsor, 1981.

Moscow, Warren. *Politics in the Empire State.* Knopf, 1948.

Nevins, Alan. *Herbert H. Lehman and His Era.* Charles Scribner's Sons, 1963.

O'Toole, Patricia. *When Trumpets Call: Theodore Roosevelt After the White House.* Simon & Schuster, 2005.

Persico, Joseph E. *The Imperial Rockefeller: A Biography of Nelson A. Rockefeller.* Simon & Schuster, 1982.

Rosenman, Samuel I. *Working with Roosevelt.* Harper & Brothers, 1952.

Slayton, Robert A. *Empire Statesman: The Rise and Redemption of Al Smith.* Free Press, 2001.

Smith, Alfred E. *Up to Now: An Autobiography.* Viking Press, 1929.

Smith, Richard Norton. *Thomas E. Dewey and His Times.* Simon & Schuster, 1982.

Stein, Leon. *The Triangle Fire.* Carroll and Graf, 1962.

Stonecash, Jeffrey M., ed. *Governing New York State.* Fourth edition. State University of New York Press, 2001.

Stonecash, Jeffrey M., John Kenneth White, and Peter W. Colby, eds. *Governing New York State.* Third edition. State University of New York Press, 1994.

Von Drehle, David. *Triangle: The Fire That Changed America.* Atlantic Monthly Press, 2003.

Ward, Robert B. *New York State Government: What It Does, How It Works.* The Rockefeller Institute Press, 2002.

INDEX